project-based learning

using information technology

SECOND EDITION

David Moursund

International Society for Technology in Education
EUGENE, OREGON • WASHINGTON, DC

project-based learning
using information technology, SECOND EDITION

David Moursund

Director of Publishing
Jean Marie Hall

Acquisitions Editor
Mathew Manweller

Production Editor
Tracy Cozzens

Layout and Production
Kim McGovern

Copy Editor
Ron Renchler, The Electronic Page

Cover Design
**Katherine Getta,
Getta Graphic Design**

Book Design
**Katherine Getta,
Getta Graphic Design**

Second Edition
ISBN 978-1-56484-196-4

Printed in the United States of America

International Society for Technology in Education (ISTE)
Washington, DC, Office:
  1710 Rhode Island Ave. NW, Suite 900, Washington, DC 20036-3132
Eugene, Oregon, Office:
  180 West 8th Ave., Suite 300, Eugene, OR 97401-2916
Order Desk: 1.800.336.5191
Order Fax: 1.541.302.3778
Customer Service: orders@iste.org
Book Publishing: books@iste.org
Book Sales and Marketing: booksmarketing@iste.org
Web: www.iste.org

about ISTE

The International Society for Technology in Education (ISTE) is the trusted source for professional development, knowledge generation, advocacy, and leadership for innovation. A nonprofit membership association, ISTE provides leadership and service to improve teaching, learning, and school leadership by advancing the effective use of technology in PK–12 and teacher education.

Home of the National Educational Technology Standards (NETS), the Center for Applied Research in Educational Technology (CARET), and the National Educational Computing Conference (NECC), ISTE represents more than 100,000 professionals worldwide. We support our members with information, networking opportunities, and guidance as they face the challenge of transforming education. To find out more about these and other ISTE initiatives, visit our website at www.iste.org.

As part of our mission, ISTE Book Publishing works with experienced educators to develop and produce practical resources for classroom teachers, teacher educators, and technology leaders. Every manuscript we select for publication is carefully peer-reviewed and professionally edited. We look for content that emphasizes the effective use of technology where it can make a difference—increasing the productivity of teachers and administrators; helping students with unique learning styles, abilities, or backgrounds; collecting and using data for decision making at the school and district levels; and creating dynamic, project-based learning environments that engage 21st-century learners. We value your feedback on this book and other ISTE products. E-mail us at books@iste.org.

about the author

Dr. David Moursund (**http://darkwing.uoregon.edu/~moursund/**) has been teaching and writing in the field of information technology in education since 1963. He was an assistant professor and then an associate professor in the Department of Mathematics and in the Computing Center (Engineering) at Michigan State University from 1963 to 1967. He was an associate professor in the Department of Mathematics and the Computing Center at the University of Oregon from 1967 to 1969. He was the chairman of the Department of Computer Science at the University of Oregon from 1969 to 1975. He is now a professor in the College of Education at the University of Oregon.

In 1974 Dr. Moursund established the *Oregon Computing Teacher*. This periodical was renamed *The Computing Teacher* in 1979 and then *Learning and Leading with Technology* in May 1995. In 1979, Dr. Moursund founded the International Council for Computers in Education (ICCE). ICCE became the International Society for Technology in Education (ISTE) in 1989 when it merged with the International Association for Computing in Education (IACE). Dr. Moursund was the executive officer of ISTE from 1989 to 1998 and was the executive officer for research and development until March 2001.

Dr. Moursund has authored or coauthored more than 30 books and numerous articles on information technology in education. He has been the dissertation director and/or served on the dissertation committee of more than 75 doctoral students in the field of computers in education. In addition, Dr. Moursund served as editor-in-chief of *Learning and Leading with Technology*, the flagship publication for ISTE, from 1974 to 2001.

Dr. Moursund currently serves as the chair of the board for the Oregon Technology in Education Council, a nonprofit, grassroots professional organization. At the same time, he continues to work for the Teacher Education Unit in the College of Education at the University of Oregon.

contents

new to this edition

Although research and theory have provided answers to many important questions related to implementing project-based education, we need to know a great deal more about how to sustain student motivation and thought in projects.

—Blumenfeld et al. (1991)

One of the constants of technology and education is that they are always changing. Newer technology comes along. Alternative educational practices are developed. The second edition of this book maintains the commitment to the theories of project-based learning but reflects the changing nature of technology and emphasizes new educational practices.

This revised edition brings a variety of new materials to the reader. In the new edition of this book you will find:

- A number of additional IT-assisted project-based learning lesson examples.

- More recent and additional research-based arguments supporting the use of project-based learning in schools.

- The incorporation of Situated Learning Theory into the practices of project-based learning.

- More emphasis on using IT-assisted project-based learning as a vehicle to teach higher-order thinking skills.

In addition, the second edition has a companion Web site created by the author (**http://darkwing.uoregon.edu/~moursund/PBL/**). It provides a continually updated annotated bibliography and detailed syllabi for workshops and short courses about IT-assisted project-based learning.

Whether you are reading about project-based learning for the first time or you have already read the first edition of this book, this new edition will provide a wealth of information about the nexus between project-based learning and information technology.

preface

This book is about project-based learning (PBL) in an information technology (IT) environment. In PBL, students produce a product, presentation, or performance. The book is designed for teachers who want to implement PBL using IT in their classrooms. Teachers who do this will learn IT alongside their students, and their students will get a better education.

PBL has long been a teaching tool of many teachers. Now, PBL is being enhanced by routine use of IT. Thus, it is now a vehicle for learning "traditional" subject matter content and for learning how to use IT effectively. The overarching goal of this book is to help students learn to use their minds (higher-order thinking and problem-solving skills) and IT (including computers, the Internet, and multimedia) effectively as they plan and carry out complex projects.

Most teachers have had experience in developing and implementing PBL lessons. IT adds three new dimensions to PBL. These new dimensions are:

- IT as an aid to carrying out the work in a project. This includes using IT in a project's product, presentation, or performance.

- IT as part of the content of a project.

- IT as a vehicle that helps create a teaching and learning environment in which students and teachers are both learners and facilitators of learning—that is, they function as a community of scholars.

This book on IT-assisted PBL is designed to help all teachers at all grade levels improve the quality of education their students receive.

Project-Based Learning

PBL is used in many schools and by many different teachers. It is not surprising that the use of PBL is growing, because PBL has a high level of "authenticity." It tends to be obvious to students, teachers, parents, and others that PBL has many adult-world characteristics and can bring concrete purpose and meaning to a wide range of school subjects. There is a growing body of research literature to support this position (see Chapter 4).

Many teachers feel that PBL is an important and effective part of their teaching repertoire. An IT-assisted PBL lesson can be viewed as an opportunity for students:

- To learn in an authentic, challenging, multidisciplinary environment.

- To learn how to design, carry out, and evaluate a project that requires sustained effort over a significant period of time.

- To learn about the topics on which the project focuses.

- To gain more IT knowledge and skills.

- To learn to work with minimal external guidance, both individually and in groups.

- To gain in self-reliance and personal accountability.

An IT-assisted PBL lesson can be viewed as an opportunity for teachers:

- To learn IT alongside their students.
- To gain skills in creating a constructivist learning environment.
- To facilitate the creation of a highly motivating learning environment.

Contents of This Book

Chapter 1, "Introduction and a PBL Example," introduces the idea of a Problem or Task Team and relates it to PBL. The chapter presents an example of IT-assisted PBL and includes a brief overview of assessment. (Chapter 7 discusses assessment in considerably more detail.)

Chapter 2, "An Overview of IT-Assisted PBL," answers the question "What is PBL?" by discussing a series of criteria that a student-centered PBL lesson usually satisfies. The chapter differentiates PBL from the more traditional, didactic, teacher-centered form of instruction.

Chapter 3, "Some PBL Lesson Topic Ideas," provides some examples of PBL lesson ideas. PBL often focuses on large and challenging problems faced by people in communities, states, nations, and the world.

Chapter 4, "The Case for PBL," presents the research literature and other arguments supporting the use of PBL in instruction.

Chapter 5, "Project Planning," covers the rudiments of what teachers and students need to know about project planning. One of the goals in PBL is for students to learn how to do the planning involved in carrying out a project.

Chapter 6, "Creating a PBL Lesson Plan," presents a detailed plan for developing a PBL lesson.

Chapter 7, "Assessment in IT-Assisted PBL," discusses student assessment in a PBL environment. It provides suggestions for assessing student work and it discusses portfolios.

Chapter 8, "The Future of IT-Assisted PBL," speculates on the future of IT-assisted PBL. As the number of computer facilities and the degree of connectivity in schools continues its rapid growth, we can expect IT-assisted PBL to become commonplace.

Appendix A, "Goals for IT in Education," is included because every IT-assisted PBL lesson is designed to help meet some IT goals. This appendix contains goals and performance indicators from ISTE's National Educational Technology Standards.

Appendix B, "An Overview of Problem Solving," is included because most IT-assisted PBL lessons have a focus on higher-order thinking skills, including problem solving.

References and Resources contains an extensive annotated collection of additional sources of information; many are Web-based materials.

Teaching and Learning Philosophy

This book is based on a philosophy of constructivist education. Constructivism assumes that a learner constructs new knowledge, building on whatever base of knowledge the learner already has. Constructivism is also a social learning theory, meaning that it involves the interactions of learners and recognizes that humans are social creatures. Learning often takes place in a group, with learners learning from each other. At the same time, learning is an individual and personal thing. No two learners bring the exact same previous knowledge and experience to a new learning situation. As every teacher knows, the range of differences among the students in a typical class is truly astonishing!

Some important educational ideas emphasized in this book include the following:

- An explicit focus by teachers and students on the transfer of learning, with explicit emphasis on the high-road, low-road theory. In addition, there is an emphasis on Situated Learning Theory. This theory emphasizes that learning takes place in a specific environment (a learning situation) and that the actual learning is highly dependent on that environment. This helps explain why learning environments should be chosen to reflect the environments to which we want students to transfer their new knowledge and skills.

- Discovery-based learning, learning by doing, active learning, being engaged

- Metacognition (thinking about one's thinking), reflection about what one is studying and learning

- Peer teaching and peer evaluation

- Authentic assessment and authentic content

- Self-assessment

- Teachable moments

- Problem solving

- Intrinsic motivation

A unifying goal is to help students gain increased expertise as independent, self-sufficient, lifelong learners.

Possible Uses of This Book

This book is specifically designed for three audiences:

1. Inservice teachers participating in workshops on IT-assisted PBL.

2. Preservice teachers enrolled in a short course or studying the materials as part of a longer course.

3. Inservice and preservice teachers who want to study on their own to learn more about PBL in an IT environment.

The book does not presuppose any specific knowledge about computers and other components of IT, PBL, or problem solving. However, it is assumed that the reader has some knowledge in all three of these areas. Appendix A provides a brief overview of the field of IT in education and goals for IT in PK–12 education. Appendix B provides an introduction to the field of problem solving, with particular emphasis on problem-solving strategies that are useful in many different disciplines. The book is designed so that individual readers will be able to build on their current knowledge and skills (demonstrating constructivism at work) as they gain new knowledge and skills.

David Moursund

CHAPTER 1

introduction and a PBL example

Even the longest journey begins with a single step.

— *Lau Tsu (570 - 490 B.C.)*

This chapter begins with a very brief introduction to information technology-assisted project-based learning (IT-assisted PBL). In IT-assisted PBL, students make effective use of IT as they produce a product, presentation, or performance. The chapter then presents an example of an IT-assisted PBL lesson and concludes with a brief discussion of some possible goals of an IT-assisted PBL lesson.

The P/T Team

PBL focuses on a problem to be solved or a task to be accomplished. The single most important idea in solving problems and accomplishing tasks is that you build on your own previous work and on the previous work of others. When faced by a challenging problem or task, you use the knowledge, skills, and aids other people have developed, as well as your own knowledge, skills, and previous work. (If this paragraph seems like Greek to you, you may want to read Appendix B, "An Overview of Problem Solving.")

Figure 1.1 illustrates a person or a group of people—a Problem or Task Team (P/T Team)—who wants to solve a complex problem or accomplish a complex task. The P/T Team draws upon three major categories of help:

1. Tools that extend mental capabilities, such as computers, conventional libraries, and the emerging Global Digital Library that we call the Web. These are sometimes called *mind tools.*

2. Tools that extend physical capabilities, such as the airplane, automobile, microscope, telescope, and telephone.

3. Our formal and informal educational system. This system provides aids to help team members build and maintain their mental and physical capabilities.

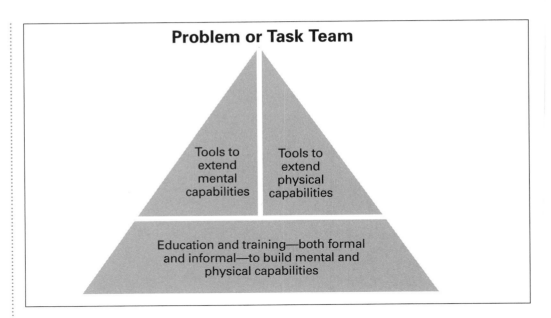

One of the major goals of education is to help students learn to solve complex problems and accomplish complex tasks. Students need to receive substantial instruction and practice in functioning in a P/T Team environment. IT-assisted PBL is specifically designed to help students learn to function in this environment.

The word "team" was carefully chosen. Even if there is only one person on the team, the team still includes a wide range of resources that other people have developed. We know a lot about how training, experience, and practice help a team become more effective. This book focuses on IT-assisted PBL as a vehicle for helping students learn to work effectively in a P/T Team environment.

The P/T Team is a unifying idea in education. Each component of education can be analyzed from the point of view of how it contributes to an individual or a group of individuals functioning in a P/T Team environment. Moreover, we can see how progress in developing better mental aids, physical aids, and educational systems can contribute to increasing the capabilities of a P/T Team.

A Sample PBL Topic—A Historical Newspaper

This section contains a brief description of an IT-assisted PBL lesson that focuses on a research, writing, and presentation task to be accomplished. The lesson can be adapted for use with students of widely varying abilities and at various grade levels. The difficulty or challenge of the task to be accomplished can be adjusted to the knowledge and skill levels of the students.

This IT-assisted PBL lesson creates a classroom environment in which the teacher learns alongside the students. As you read through the following lesson plan ideas, think what you might learn from your students as they carry out the PBL lesson.

The class is divided into teams of three to four students, who carry out these activities:

1. Each team selects an important historical date (or event) between 50 and 150 years in the past.

2. Each team selects a city.

3. Each team produces a newspaper that might have been published and distributed shortly after the historical date in the city selected. The newspaper is to be desktop published in a historically authentic style. The team selects a name for the newspaper and has collective responsibility for the overall quality of the design, layout, desktop publishing, and content of the text and graphics in the newspaper.

4. Each team member selects a particular content area or section of the newspaper and is responsible for writing the content for that area or section. Some examples of content areas or sections of the newspaper include:

   • The historical event itself—news, editorials, and human-interest stories about the event

   • World news

   • National news

   • Local and regional news

   • Sports

   • Music

   • Arts

   • Literature (for example, a book review of a recently published book)

   • Science in the news

   • Ads

5. Each team member provides formative evaluation feedback on both the content and writing done by each team member.

6. Each team publishes eight copies of its newspaper so that each team member gets a copy to take home, the teacher gets two copies, and a couple of copies are left for circulation to the other teams.

7. At the end of the project, each team makes a presentation to the whole class. It covers both the processes the team carried out and the product the team produced.

8. Students are assessed in five major areas:

   • Historical research (20%)

   • Writing (30%)

   • Cooperative/collaborative project work in a P/T Team environment (20%)

   • Design and desktop publication (15%)

   • Final presentation (15%)

This is a very open-ended assignment. More detail is needed before students can get started. Here are some examples of the types of questions that need to be addressed:

   • How much class time each day and how many days will be devoted to this project?

   • How will the teams be selected? (Will the teacher assign members to the teams or do the students themselves form the teams?)

   • How will the individual students and teams be assessed?

- Can two teams select the same historical event or the same city?

- What will be in the presentations to the class at the end of the project and how much time will be available for a presentation? Will each team member do part of the presentation? What media can be used in the presentation?

- What if I (a student) don't like any of the topics you (the teacher) have named? (Answer: The student can select any content area/section that might have been in a newspaper of that date.)

- If I really like to draw, is it all right if I do the artwork for the articles that the other members of my team are writing—and not write an article myself? (This is an example of a student pushing the limits. If one goal of the project is to have students practice their research and writing skills, then the answer is "no." A compromise might be that the student can do an article on political cartoons of the time period. The article could be well illustrated with the student's drawings.)

There are many other questions that might arise, for example, "How long does the newspaper need to be?" or "How long does my article need to be?" You may deliberately choose to not answer some of these questions. From a teacher's point of view, you want the individual teams and students to push themselves. Indeed, you might want to promote a spirit of competition among teams. You want an appropriate balance between quality and quantity. You want the articles to have authentic, well-researched content. You want each individual student to expend sustained effort throughout the project. Some students will write multiple articles. Others may spend a great deal of time researching and developing a single article. Some teams will spend a lot of time preparing their presentations and may "wow" the class.

A major PBL lesson should end with the whole class participating in a debriefing session. What were the good and not-so-good features of the project? What would make it a more valuable learning experience to individual students and to the whole class? What new projects are suggested by the work that has been done? Would the class recommend that this same assignment be used with next year's class?

Many PBL lessons can be used year after year, perhaps with only minor revisions. A good PBL lesson may have offshoots, or variations, that can be used in future lessons. Here are several extensions and variations on the historical newspaper lesson:

1. The teacher selects the historical event, and each team develops a newspaper for that historical event and time period. The teacher might select an event within "recent" history so that students can interview local citizens who were alive at the time of the event. This would give students the opportunity to practice the study of oral history.

2. Each student writes two or more articles for the team newspaper. One article discusses the historical event; the other is on a different topic the student selects.

3. Instead of doing a formal presentation to the whole class, each team develops a presentation for a poster session. This is akin to the poster sessions one often sees at conferences. Each team develops a large display representing its contribution to the project. Team members might bring in historical artifacts or develop replicas of historical artifacts. Teams then interact with small groups of students who visit and explore each poster session presentation.

4. Suppose the historical event being written about is of historical significance in several countries. (Wars, for example, have this characteristic.) Students from several different countries could simultaneously carry out this same assignment. A major component of the overall PBL lesson in this case is for students to compare, contrast, and understand the differing points of view represented by the student writers from different countries.

Hardware and Software Requirements

This book focuses on PBL in an IT environment. The suggested classroom activities can be carried out using whatever IT is available in the school, home, and community environment. A school need not have the latest, greatest, and best IT facilities.

However, there is an underlying hardware and software goal that this book supports. Students need to learn to make routine, everyday use of IT as an aid to carrying out projects. The general type of hardware and software that students need and/or should be routinely using includes:

- Generic tools, such as word processors, spreadsheets, databases, and paint and draw software. Generic tools cut across all academic disciplines, much in the same way that reading, writing, and arithmetic cut across all disciplines. These generic tools may be included in an integrated software package or may be individual pieces of software.

- Hypermedia software and hardware, including devices such as scanners, digital cameras, video cameras, and VCRs, as well as the connectivity and software needed to use these devices. Hypermedia software makes it possible for students to learn to read and write nonlinear, interactive documents that contain text, sound, graphics, and video.

- Connectivity to the Internet and World Wide Web.

- Desktop-publishing hardware and software. (Generic software and a printer will usually suffice.)

- Desktop presentation hardware and software, including projection facilities.

- Hardware with adequate speed and reliability. The quality of the hardware should not impede its use. (Hardware that is "down" or "flacky" impedes its use.)

In many classrooms, some of this hardware and software is not yet available. However, this should not be used as a barrier to engaging students in IT-assisted PBL. The key idea is that whatever the students have available can be used in PBL. While part of an IT-assisted PBL lesson may focus on the hardware and software, the more important and long-lasting learning components focus on topics that are relatively independent of any specific hardware and software.

Some teachers feel that a student must learn a great deal about a particular computer tool before beginning to use it in a PBL project. This book takes the opposite tack. Its premise is that with a minimum of knowledge about a computer tool, a student can begin to use it to carry out a project. The project then serves as a motivational experience and provides an authentic context for learning more about the tool. Learning about the tool and using the tool to carry out a project are thoroughly integrated.

Similarly, some teachers feel that they themselves must know a great deal about a wide range of computer tools before beginning to engage their students in IT-assisted PBL. Indeed, many teachers find that this is a convenient excuse for not getting started in using IT-assisted PBL. Many other teachers have found that once they get started (no matter how small their initial IT knowledge) they learn on the job. They learn from their students and they learn by doing. This book strongly supports such an approach.

In PBL, a great deal of peer instruction occurs. This is especially true in an IT environment. All students can and should learn to help their peers and others learn about IT and how to use IT in carrying out a project. Indeed, peer instruction and peer assessment can be a component of every IT-assisted PBL lesson.

The Goals of IT-Assisted PBL

An IT-assisted PBL lesson has multiple goals for students. Typically, these include the following:

1. Developing content area expertise. The goal of the project is for students to increase their knowledge and skill within a discipline or an interdisciplinary content area. By doing a project, students often gain a high level of expertise within the specific area they are studying. A student may become the most knowledgeable person in the class on a specific topic. Indeed, a student's level of knowledge within a narrow domain may come to exceed the teacher's level of knowledge.

2. Improving research skills. The project requires the use of research skills, thus helping students improve their skills in this area.

3. Improving higher-order thinking skills. The project is challenging and focuses on helping students improve their higher-order thinking skills.

4. Learning how to do a project. The project helps students increase their knowledge and skill in undertaking a challenging project that requires sustained effort over a considerable period of time. A team of students will often work on a project; therefore, students learn to take individual and collective responsibility for the team's successful completion of the project. Students learn from each other.

5. Learning to use IT. Students increase their knowledge and skill in using IT while working on a project. A project may include the specific goal of assisting students in acquiring new knowledge and skills in IT.

6. Conducting self-assessment and peer assessment. Students gain skill in assessing themselves and being accountable for their own work and performance. They learn how to assess the work and performance of their peers and provide them with useful feedback.

7. Developing a portfolio. The project requires students to produce a product, presentation, or performance that is of portfolio quality. The project may become part of the student's portfolio for the school year, and it may even become part of the student's long-term portfolio.

8. Assuming personal responsibility for one's engagement in a relatively complex learning task. Students are actively and appropriately engaged in carrying out the work of the project; thus, they are intrinsically motivated. This is a process goal. As a teacher, you might make daily observations that determine whether students are on task, whether they are showing exemplary cooperative behavior, or whether they are displaying disruptive behavior. You might require your students to keep a daily log of their specific work on and contributions to a team project, and ask them to turn this log in each week.

9. Being a part of a community of scholars. The entire class—student, teacher, teaching assistants, and volunteers—becomes a community of scholars, working together and learning from each other. This community of scholars often expands to include parents, students from outside the class, and others.

10. Working on important ideas. The project should focus on important ideas and continuing themes emphasized by the teacher, school, or school district. For example, communication, math competence, and interdisciplinary problem solving may be goals in every project.

A good IT-assisted PBL lesson is likely to include most of these goals, which, along with other major process goals and learning goals, provide a framework for evaluation and assessment. And don't forget—as a teacher you should have personal learning goals in every PBL assignment. At the end of the lesson, spend some time analyzing what you learned.

Some Additional Important Ideas

The following list provides a brief introduction to three other important ideas related to PBL. These topics are treated in more detail in subsequent chapters of this book.

1. PBL is learner centered. Students have a significant voice in selecting the content areas and nature of the projects they do. There is considerable focus on ensuring that students understand what it is they are doing, why it is important, and how they will be assessed. Indeed, students may help set some of the goals on which they will be assessed and the method of assessment that will be used.

   All of these learner-centered characteristics of PBL contribute to learner motivation and active engagement. A high level of intrinsic motivation and active engagement is essential to the success of a PBL lesson.

2. PBL is problem or task oriented. In very simple terms, much of education concerns helping students (a) gain some basic knowledge and skills and (b) learn to solve challenging problems and accomplish challenging tasks using their knowledge and skills.

   The terms *lower order* and *higher order* are often applied to the knowledge and skills that are central to achieving these two overarching educational goals. Both types of knowledge and skills are essential to being an educated person. Thus, educators and others are understandably concerned about the relative emphasis that should be placed on each type, as well as which type should come first. Educational leaders generally conclude that most lessons should contain an emphasis on both lower-order and higher-order knowledge and skills. That is, lower-order knowledge and skills should be gained in the context of solving challenging problems and accomplishing challenging tasks.

   In a PBL lesson, a unifying goal is for students to work on solving a challenging problem or accomplishing a challenging task. Every PBL lesson should include an emphasis on higher-order knowledge and skills.

3. Authentic assessment is an important component of PBL. Students need to have a clear understanding of the goals, evaluation, and assessment in a project. Learning about these areas is part of the process of learning how to undertake projects. Keep in mind that authentic assessment and authentic curriculum content are closely related topics (Wiggins, 1993a, 1993b).

It is important to distinguish between feedback (formative evaluation) and assessment. During a project, students may receive formative evaluation (feedback) from themselves, their peers, their teacher, and other sources. This feedback helps students learn, and it helps them produce a high-quality final product, presentation, or performance. While some teachers will use this formative evaluation information in grading (assessing) a student, others will base assessment mainly on the final product. A student is usually assessed both on the process and the product. Keep in mind that a good learning environment allows students to experiment, to try things that may not turn out to be successful. A good assessment system should encourage and reward such trial and error, rather than punish it.

PBL Research and Testimonials

The research and underlying theory supporting the value of IT-assisted PBL are strong but not overwhelmingly strong. (Chapter 4 discusses research and theory in more detail.) Moreover, IT-assisted PBL presents many challenges to teachers and our educational system. Assessment (discussed in Chapter 7) is another major issue. In addition, many teachers find that they need inservice education to help them increase their comfort level when initially using IT-assisted PBL.

Some of the material included in this is book has been presented in a number of workshops for inservice teachers. These presentations never fail to evoke testimonials from teachers who use PBL in their teaching. Invariably, several workshop participants will tell the group that using PBL is an important part of their teaching repertoire and that they will never go back to "traditional" teaching. Often their testimonials are impassioned—the teachers have become true believers in this style of teaching.

Many teachers teach in environments where a heavy emphasis is placed on students doing well on national or state tests. These tests often emphasize lower-order knowledge and skills. Teachers know that they can help their students achieve higher test scores if they specifically teach to the tests. They also know that much of this test-oriented knowledge and skill does not stick with the student—that is, it has little lasting value. Veteran PBL teachers feel that their students learn and retain the basics because they learn and practice their basics in an authentic environment. There is a growing collection of research that supports this contention.

Activities

1. Many people benefit from keeping a journal as they work their way through a book such as this. In the journal, they reflect on ideas that occur to them as they read. For example, as you read this first chapter, did you think about how PBL was used when you were an elementary or secondary school student? If you are currently a teacher, did you think about how you have used PBL in your teaching?

    A. Start a journal. Begin by discussing the idea of the P/T Team. Does this seem like an important idea? How would you convince a parent or a school board member that this is an important idea in education?

    B. Make some entries in your journal each time you read a chapter or part of a chapter. From time to time you may want to go back to previous entries and write additional comments.

2. Think about a PBL lesson you experienced while you were a student. Describe and analyze the project, identifying its strengths and weaknesses. What did you learn by doing the project? Why are you still able to remember this project from the past?

3. Analyze the historical newspaper project described in this chapter. What are its strengths and weaknesses? Suggest some ways to overcome the weaknesses.

4. Consider the 10 IT-assisted PBL lesson goals given in this chapter.

   A. Which of these 10 general goals would you emphasize in the historical newspaper project, and why?

   B. For the goals you pick in 4A, what percentages (totaling 100%) would you assign to each? How would you actually do these assessments? Explain how your assessment methods would be valid, reliable, and fair to all students.

an overview of IT-assisted PBL

Knowledge is of two kinds.
We know a subject ourselves,
or we know where we can find
information upon it.

— *Samuel Johnson (1709 – 1784)*

This chapter contains an overview of PBL in an IT environment. It also discusses the teaching concept of "sage on the stage" versus "guide on the side." PBL and IT-assisted PBL represent a considerably different approach to teaching than the more commonly used "stand and deliver."

What Is PBL?

The historical newspaper example from Chapter 1 illustrates a number of the features common to many IT-assisted PBL lessons. However, it is important to understand that there is no universally agreed upon definition of what constitutes PBL. Almost all teachers use some PBL, and the projects they use vary widely in form and content.

This book focuses specifically on PBL that is designed to be carried out in an IT environment. Sometimes the focus of the lesson will be mostly on IT. Very often, however, one of the lesser goals will be an increase in IT knowledge and skills among students participating in the lesson.

Project-based learning is sometimes called problem-based learning, and vice versa. In problem-based learning, the focus is on a specific problem to be addressed. For example, the problem might be to clean up a polluted stream running through one's city, or to save an endangered species of plant or animal. Problem-based learning is common in business education and medical education. The References and Resources section of this book contains information on both project-based learning and problem-based learning.

Project-based learning constitutes a broader category of instruction than problem-based learning. While a project may address a specific problem, it can also focus on areas that are not problems. A key characteristic of project-based learning is that the project does not focus on learning about something. It focuses on doing something. It is action oriented. In the historical newspaper example, students are doing research, doing writing, doing peer feedback, doing the design of a historically authentic newspaper, doing desktop publication, and doing a presentation to the whole class.

PBL from a Student's Point of View

As the following list demonstrates, PBL can be analyzed in at least six ways from a student's point of view. (Of course, some of the items in the list might fit equally well in the list in the next major section, "PBL from a Teacher's Point of View.") Considered from a student's viewpoint, PBL:

1. Is learner centered and intrinsically motivating.

2. Encourages collaboration and cooperative learning.

3. Allows students to make incremental and continual improvement in their products, presentations, or performances.

4. Is designed so that students are actively engaged in doing things rather than in learning about something.

5. Requires students to produce a product, presentation, or performance.

6. Is challenging, with a focus on higher-order skills.

Each of these characteristics is briefly discussed in the six sections that follow.

Learner Centered, Intrinsically Motivating

- Students have considerable choice of topics, as well as the nature and extent of the content of the project. The learning environment is designed to help students be intrinsically motivated as they shape their projects to fit their own interests and abilities. A student may need to put substantial time and effort into defining the specific project to be carried out. The product, presentation, or production the student produces has a personal touch—it represents the student.

- Essentially the same project assignment can be given to students of considerably different academic backgrounds, grade levels, and academic abilities. Students construct new knowledge and skills, building on their current knowledge and skills. Constructivism is one of the key learning theories underlying PBL.

- Students conduct research using multiple sources of information, such as books, the Web, videotapes, personal interviews (conducted in person or through telecommunications), and their own experiments. Even if their projects are based on the same topic, different students will probably use considerably different sources of information.

- Students are included in the development of the assessment and have a full understanding of it. They learn to assess their own work and to have confidence in the accuracy and value of self-assessment.

Collaboration and Cooperative Learning

- A team of people may work on the project. The team may be an entire class, several classes, or even students from several remote sites. In these cases, individuals or small groups work on different components of a large task, and their joint collaborative efforts are often coordinated through technology. Multisite projects often rely on e-mail or videoconferencing.

- Peer instruction is explicitly taught and encouraged. Students learn to learn from each other and learn how to help their peers learn.

- Students learn to assess the work of their peers. They learn to provide constructive feedback to themselves and to their peers.

Incremental and Continual Improvement

- The definition of what is to be accomplished as well as the actual components and products in the project allows for continual revision and incremental improvement during the project.

- A project is viewed as a process rather than as a product. A strong parallel exists between process-based writing and PBL. One of the keys to good writing is "revise, revise, revise." As work on the project proceeds, the project itself and the work to be done on it is under continual review and may undergo substantial change.

- A project has time limitations. Thus, students must make decisions about how to use their time. If too much time is spent developing and improving one component, the other components may not be of high quality, so the overall project may suffer. One of the goals in a typical PBL lesson is to have students learn to make the necessary decisions about producing an appropriate level of quality under the existing time constraints.

Actively Engaged Students

- In PBL classrooms, the average noise level is much higher than in traditional classrooms because students often work in groups. Thus, conversations, movement, sharing, and helping each other is the norm.

- The teacher circulates within the classroom, interacting briefly with individuals and groups, providing feedback and help as appropriate. The teacher functions as a "guide on the side" rather than as a "sage on the stage." Thus, students learn to be more self-reliant and how to work in cooperative, collaborative groups They learn to seek help from each other or to figure out things for themselves.

Product, Presentation, or Performance

- The project involves the design and development of a product, presentation, or performance that others can use or view. A product might be an artifact or exhibit, for example, a display at a science fair. It might be a written product or an interactive hypermedia product. A performance might be a skit, play, or musical performance. Students may present the results of their projects in class as reports or posters. Other projects may extend beyond the school boundaries in the form of stage or broadcast performances, publications, and public events. Students may create products of significant and lasting value, such as environmental assessments or permanent information displays.

- A project may result in a product, presentation, or performance that becomes a component of a student's portfolio. In IT-assisted PBL, the product, presentation, or performance may be in electronic format and become part of an electronic portfolio.

Challenging, with a Focus on Higher-Order Skills

- There is a focus on higher-order skills, including problem solving, independent research, setting one's own goals, and self-monitoring (self-assessment).

- The project is designed to facilitate learning and learning to learn. Each student is immersed in a rich learning environment that includes feedback from self, peers, teachers, and others. Students are expected to stretch their knowledge and skills. They are expected to gain skills as independent, self-sufficient learners.

- The process of doing a project allows and encourages students to experiment, to do discovery-based learning, to learn from their mistakes, and to encounter and overcome unexpected and difficult challenges.

PBL from a Teacher's Point of View

PBL can also be analyzed from a teacher's point of view. Typically, a project extends over a significant period of time, perhaps from several weeks to an entire school year. Thus, a PBL lesson can be viewed as a major unit of study. Considered from a teacher's point of view, PBL:

1. Has authentic content and purpose, with a major emphasis on higher-order thinking and problem solving.

2. Uses authentic assessment.

3. Is teacher facilitated (but the teacher is much more of a "guide on the side" than a "sage on the stage").

4. Has explicit educational goals.

5. Is rooted in constructivism (a social learning theory).

6. Is designed to facilitate transfer of learning.

7. Is designed so that the teacher will be a learner.

Each of these ideas is briefly discussed in the six sections that follow.

Authentic Content and Purpose

- The context for the subject matter tends to be complex and authentic. (It is "real-world" in the sense that it is similar to problems and tasks that adults address.) Many projects focus on a specific current problem, such as an environmental or social problem. The purpose of such projects is for students to make a contribution toward solving the problems. Such problems are complex and do not have simple solutions.

- One goal of the project is to help students get better at defining and carrying out projects in which there are limited resources. You want your students to gain increased skill in budgeting resources (such as their own time) and taking personal responsibility for completing the project on time.

- The project usually cuts across a number of disciplines. Students are expected to draw upon their full range of knowledge and skills.

- The project requires students to do research that draws on multiple sources of information. These sources may be complex and contain contradictory information. Many projects require empirical research.

- The project is consistent with and supportive of the general goals of education as well as the specific goals and objectives of the subject matter the teacher is responsible for teaching.

Authentic Assessment

- The overall assessment of student work is authentic. Authentic assessment is sometimes called "performance assessment," and it may include the assessment of a student's portfolio. In authentic assessment, students are expected to solve challenging problems and accomplish challenging tasks. The emphasis is on higher-order thinking skills. In the same sense that the curriculum content in PBL is authentic and real-world like, the authentic assessment is a direct measure of student performance and knowledge of the authentic content. Students have a clear understanding of the assessment guidelines, and assessment is guided by and directed toward the product, presentation, or performance developed during the project. (Chapter 7 contains more information about assessment in PBL.)

- In PBL, students learn to do self-assessment and peer assessment. (They are given specific, directed instruction on how to provide effective, constructive feedback to their peers, and they repeatedly practice this task.)

- The product, presentation, or performance often becomes part of the student's hardcopy portfolio or electronic portfolio.

Teacher Facilitated

- The teacher acts as a facilitator, mentor, and consultant, providing resources and advice to students as they pursue their investigations. However, the students collect and analyze the information, make discoveries, and report their results. The teacher is not the primary delivery system of information. Indeed, a specific PBL goal is to help students become more self-sufficient learners.

- The instruction and facilitation is guided by a broad range of explicit teaching goals. Some of these goals may be narrowly focused on specific subject matter content. Other goals will probably be more broadly based, interdisciplinary, or discipline independent. For example, there is explicit teaching for transfer of learning. (Transfer of learning is discussed later is this section and in Appendix B, "An Overview of Problem Solving.") Students will achieve additional (unforeseen) goals as they explore complex topics from a variety of perspectives.

- The teacher looks for and acts on "teachable moments." This often involves calling the whole class together to learn about and discuss a particular (perhaps unexpected) situation that one student or a team of students has encountered.

- The teacher is in charge of the class. The teacher has the authority and bears the ultimate responsibility for curriculum, instruction, and assessment. The teacher uses the tools and methodology of authentic assessment and must face and overcome the challenge that each student is constructing his or her own new knowledge rather than studying the same content as the other students.

Explicit Educational Goals

- The project is designed to facilitate learning. It is designed to help achieve the overall goals of education. It includes a focus on specific educational goals, often cutting across several disciplines.

- An explicit goal in every project is to improve the students' ability to function effectively in a P/T Team environment. If the project is being carried out by a multiperson team, then learning to be an effective member of a team is an explicit goal of the project.

- In IT-assisted PBL, the project is designed to help students learn about IT and use it effectively in carrying out a project.

- The project is designed to help increase the students' ability to carry out complex, challenging, real-world projects.

Rooted in Constructivism, but Uses Multiple Methods of Instruction

- The design of the curriculum, instruction, and assessment is rooted in constructivism. Constructivism is a theory of knowledge and learning based on the idea that individual learners construct their own knowledge, building on their current knowledge.

- Students are provided time for reflection about what they are learning. They often use journals for this metacognitive activity.

- An IT-assisted PBL lesson will usually include some direct, explicit (didactic) instruction. Often this will occur when the teacher encounters a teachable moment—a problem encountered by an individual student or a team of students, where the whole class would benefit from explicit instruction.

Facilitates Transfer of Learning

- Students are given specific instruction about the idea of transfer of learning.

- In PBL, students are strongly encouraged to draw upon their knowledge from many different fields and apply the new knowledge and skills they are learning in many different fields.

- Following the general ideas of situated learning theory, PBL lessons and their supporting learning environments are specifically designed to facilitate learning that transfers to real-world settings.

Teacher as Learner

- The teacher is also a learner. The teacher and the students learn together, and the teacher models the role of being a lifelong learner.

- The teacher allocates time to reflect on his or her own learning.

- The teacher may do action research and/or journaling to facilitate personal learning during a PBL lesson.

Didactic Versus Constructivist Teaching

The Industrial Revolution began in England in the late 1700s. It led to a mass movement of people from the farms into the cities. As families were attracted to the cities to work in the factories, the problem arose as to what to do with the children. There are innumerable tasks (learning by doing) that are appropriate for young children on a farm. This was especially true before the development of current highly mechanized forms of farming.

A solution to this problem was to develop public schools and require all children to attend. The schools that developed had many characteristics of factories. Students were assumed to be nearly alike. All students in a class were assumed to be ready to learn the new topics specified in the curriculum. The teacher presented the information to be learned, drilled students to facilitate memorization, and tested the students. This type of teaching is often described as didactic instruction or direct instruction.

This didactic, factory model of education gradually spread throughout the world. It has persisted for nearly 200 years and is still the dominant model of instruction in most schools. In this form of instruction, the teacher is often characterized as being a "sage on the stage," and functioning in a "stand and deliver" mode."

Constructivism is a learning theory that assumes a learner constructs new knowledge, building on whatever base of knowledge the learner already has. Constructivism is a relatively new learning theory, although it is rooted in the work of Dewey and Piaget done many years ago. Constructivism is based on our steadily increasing understanding of the human brain—how it stores and retrieves information, how it learns, and how learning builds on and extends previous learning. In instruction based on constructivism, the teacher is often characterized as being a "guide on the side."

Few teachers teach in a purely didactic manner or in a purely constructivist manner. Almost all teachers use both approaches, switching from one to the other as seems appropriate at the time. However, didactic and constructivist instruction represent two quite different philosophies of instruction and theories of learning. Figure 2.1 is designed to identify the differences between these two approaches to teaching and learning. The table is an extension of ideas presented in Sandholtz, Ringstaff, and Dwyer (1997, p. 14). The listed topics are grouped into three areas: Curriculum, Instruction, and Assessment. There is substantial overlap among these three categories, so in many cases the assignment to a particular category is somewhat arbitrary.

FIGURE 2.1

Comparing didactic and constructivist instruction.

CURRICULUM		
Educational Component	**Didactic Curriculum**	**Constructivist-Based Curriculum**
Concept of knowledge	Facts. Memorization. Discipline specific. Lower-order thinking skills.	Relationships. Inquiry and invention. Higher-order thinking skills. Represent and solve complex problems, drawing on multiple resources over an extended period of time.
IT as content	Taught in specific time blocks or courses that focus on IT.	Integrated into all content areas, as well as being a content area in its own right.
IT as tool	IT facilities available in a computer lab or library. Use not integrated into everyday activities.	IT facilities available in the classroom as well as elsewhere. Use is integrated into the routine of the class day.
Information sources	Teacher, textbooks, traditional reference books and CD-ROMs, use of a limited library, controlled access to other information.	All previously available information sources. Access to people and information through the Internet and the Web.
Information-processing aids	Paper, pencil, and ruler. Mind.	All previously available aids to information processing. Calculator, computer, computerized instruments.
Time schedule	Careful adherence to prescribed amounts of time each day on specific disciplines.	Time scheduling is flexible, making possible extended blocks of time to spend on a project.
Problem solving. Higher-order thinking skills.	Students work alone on problems presented in textbooks. Problems are usually of limited scope. Modest emphasis on higher-order thinking skills. Students tend to equate the word "problem" with "math problem."	Students work individually and collaboratively on multidisciplinary problems. Problems are typically broad in scope, and students pose or help pose the problems. Substantial emphasis on higher-order thinking skills.
Curriculum	Focus on a specific discipline and a specific, precharted pathway through the curriculum.	Curriculum is usually interdisciplinary, without a precharted pathway. Different students study different curriculums.

FIGURE 2.1
(Continued)

Comparing didactic and
constructivist instruction.

INSTRUCTION		
Educational Component	**Didactic Curriculum**	**Constructivist-Based Curriculum**
Classroom activity	Teacher centered. Teacher driven. Teacher is responsible for "covering" a set curriculum.	Learner centered (student centered). Cooperative. Interactive. Student has increased responsibility for learning. Collaborative tasks. Teams.
Teacher role	Dispenser of knowledge. Expert. Fully in charge. Gatekeeper.	Collaborator, facilitator, consultant, learner.
Teacher-student interaction	Teacher lectures and asks questions, student recites.	Teacher works with groups, facilitating PBL. Students and teachers ask and answer deeper, longer questions.
Technology use	Computer-assisted learning (drill and practice, tutorial, simulations). Tools used for amplification. Synchronous Distance Learning, designed to emulate a traditional didactic classroom.	Communication, collaboration, information access, information processing, multimedia documents and presentations. Asynchronous distance learning, often focusing on topics selected by the learner.
Instruction	Lecture/demonstration with quick recall and student recitation of facts. Seatwork, quizzes, and exams. Single-discipline oriented. "Sage on the stage."	"Guide on the side." Mentoring. Discovery-based learning. Peer instruction. Interdisciplinary oriented.
Parent and home role; community	Help on or encouragement for doing homework. Support of "traditional" education.	Parents and students learn from each other. Parents contribute to projects. Home technology supplements school technology.
Physical layout of classroom	Chairs arranged in rows in a fixed format. Chairs may be bolted to the floor.	Movable furniture to facilitate easy regroupings of furniture and students.

FIGURE 2.1
(Continued)

Comparing didactic and
constructivist instruction.

ASSESSMENT		
Educational Component	**Didactic Curriculum**	**Constructivist-Based Curriculum**
Student role as a learner	Listener (often passive). Quiet, well behaved. Raises hand when prepared to respond to a teacher's question. Studies directed toward passing tests and completing required work.	Collaborator, teacher, peer evaluator, sometimes expert. Actively engaged. Active learning. Problem poser. Active seeker after knowledge. Students learn as they help each other learn.
Demonstration of success	Quantity and speed of recall. Ability to do well on standard tests.	Quality of understanding. Ability to transfer knowledge and skills to new and novel settings.
Use of technology during assessment	Allows simple tools, such as paper, pencil, and ruler. Sometimes allows calculator.	Students assessed in environment in which they learn.
Student work-products	Most student work-products are written and private, shared only with the teacher. Occasional oral presentation.	Most student work-products are public, subject to review by teachers, peers, parents, and others. Multiple forms of products.
Assessment	Norm referenced. Objective and short answer. Focus on memorization of facts. Discipline specific. Lower-order thinking skills.	Criterion referenced. Authentic assessment of products, performances, and presentations. Portfolio. Self-assessment. Peer assessment.

Activities

1. Select an example of PBL you have experienced as a student or facilitated as a teacher. Describe this example and analyze it from the point of view of the student-oriented and teacher-oriented characteristics of IT-assisted PBL described in this chapter. What are its strengths and weaknesses?

2. Analyze your own teaching from a didactic versus constructivist point of view. From your point of view, what are the strengths and weaknesses of these two approaches to teaching? In your teaching, how do you capitalize on these strengths and avoid the weaknesses?

3. Analyze your current curriculum, instruction, and assessment in terms of how well they contribute to your students learning to function well in a P/T Team environment. Suggest some changes that might contribute to your students gaining increased knowledge and skills in solving problems and accomplishing tasks in this environment.

CHAPTER 3
some PBL lesson topic ideas

Simple things should be simple.
Complex things should be simple.

— Alan Kay (1941–)

Many teachers ask, "Where can I find some good ideas for PBL lessons?" In brief, good ideas and suitable topics are everywhere. Look at what is current and relevant to the lives of your students. Look at the big problems facing the world now and historically. Look at the problems your students' parents faced. Look at the major content ideas you want to cover in your curriculum. This chapter will help you find ideas for PBL lessons.

The Chicken and the Egg

Which comes first—an important curriculum idea that might be well taught using IT-assisted PBL, or an IT-assisted PBL lesson idea that might be adapted to one's curriculum?

Most teachers work in both directions. In brief:

1. When you have an important curriculum idea or standard you want to cover, make a list of the curriculum goals you want to achieve. Then think about the various teaching methodologies at your disposal. Select a teaching methodology that is best aligned with your curriculum goals. If you have not used much IT-assisted PBL in the past, be venturesome. Conduct some experiments to help you learn effective uses of IT-assisted PBL and make this methodology part of your teaching repertoire.

2. Through your reading, talking with your fellow teachers, attending workshops, and so on, look for PBL lessons that have been successful. Think about how these might be adapted to fit your particular teaching situation. If you are trying to increase your knowledge and skills in using PBL, you might want to begin by adapting a PBL lesson that has worked well for others.

The previous chapter summarized characteristics of a good PBL lesson from a student's point of view and a teacher's point of view. In brief, the content should be authentic, challenging, and learner centered. The focus should be on having students pose challenging problems and tasks, and then working to solve problems or accomplish tasks. Keep these ideas in mind as you examine the topic ideas given in this chapter.

A Heartfelt Need or Concern

To the greatest extent possible, you want your students to have ownership of the projects they undertake. You want them to define a problem or task for which they have a heartfelt need or concern. You want them to be intrinsically motivated to work on the project. Thus, at the beginning of a project, you want to provide them with adequate time and appropriate guidance as they make the choices that will define their individual or team projects.

The upside of students being intrinsically motivated is that they may well accomplish far more than you would have imagined. They will push themselves; they will grow; they will achieve their potential.

However, there are possible downsides. For example, one section of this chapter discusses a project in which students explore architectural and environmental barriers to learning. Suppose your students find that their classroom and school are beset by major architectural and environmental problems. What happens if your students call a press conference, write a letter to the school board and the mayor, or enlist the aid of a lawyer (perhaps a parent of one of your students) to bring a suit against the school district?

Both the upside and downside of projects should be discussed openly with your students. You may want to establish ground rules about allowable actions they can take. The development of such ground rules can be a whole-class component of the overall project.

Holiday Greeting Cards

The Holiday Greeting Cards project involves preparing and mailing out a large number of holiday greeting cards or letters to one's friends and acquaintances. Spend a minute thinking through this project. It involves these activities:

1. Creating a mailing list or adapting an existing address list. What addresses need to be added or deleted? How can one update addresses that have changed since the last time the list was used? (A computer database can be used for developing and maintaining the mailing list.)

2. Generating content. Will everybody receive the same commercially produced card? Will there be a newsletter enclosed? If so, the newsletter needs to be written and copied. (Creating a newsletter is a nice IT-component.) Will there be personal notes added for some people?

3. Selecting materials. Paper, cards, envelopes, return-address stickers, and stamps will be needed.

4. Addressing and stuffing the envelopes. Make sure the material to be included in the envelope is supposed to go to the addressee. (Perhaps mail-merge software can be used effectively in this part of the project.)

5. Affixing stamps and writing the return address. This is a relatively mechanical, nonthinking task. As students work on a project, help them recognize these kinds of tasks, which tend to get automated. Machines can do them faster, cheaper, and more accurately than people.

Notice that many of the steps require careful thought. The overall project requires planning and allocation of resources. What will it cost? How long will it take? How much individual personalization is desirable, and how will it be achieved? When do the envelopes need to go into the mail? This project requires a sustained effort, perhaps over a considerable period of time.

There are variations on the project that make it still more complex. For example, suppose the students in the class collectively decide to develop a holiday newsletter, with each student writing a part of it. This adds a new dimension of collaborative writing and desktop publishing.

One important role the teacher plays in a PBL lesson is in helping students see the parallels between the project and similar real-world projects. There is a strong parallel between this mailing activity done by students and what a business does as it prepares and sends a mass mailing to its customers. The business mailing may involve billing customers, or it may involve advertising products and services.

Preparing and implementing mass mailings is such a routine component of business that many business employees work full time on these tasks. This is an area of business that has been highly automated. The databases are stored on computers. A computer program checks the mailing addresses and ZIP codes against a master file provided by the Postal Service. Bills are generated by computers. Advertising materials are developed using computers for writing and design, and are then published using desktop-publishing hardware and software. Materials are printed using high-speed presses. Envelopes are stuffed using automated equipment. The Postal Service makes substantial use of IT in processing and delivering the mail.

Here are a couple of variations on this project:

1. An alternative to using stamps and envelopes to deliver greeting cards is to deliver them by e-mail.

2. Do a whole-class project to develop an international list of "penpals" with whom the class will share holiday greetings. This project includes learning about whether the holiday even exists in various other countries, and how it is celebrated. The information gained in this study can be shared with the individuals on the penpal list.

The Architectural Environment of the Classroom

Take a look at the classroom in which you teach. It is also the classroom in which your students learn. Is this classroom well designed for teaching and learning? Is it a pleasant place to be? You and your students spend a lot of hours in this classroom. What would make it better?

The term "environment" has many different meanings. For example, it is used in talking about nature and water pollution. It is used in talking about the social environment of a community or a school, and it is used in talking about a physical or architectural setting.

This specific example focuses on the architectural environment, including such elements as access, heat, light, air quality, and space. A school and its classrooms, playgrounds, and other physical spaces should be designed to help the school accomplish its mission.

How are teaching and learning affected by a school's architectural environment? For example, is learning adversely affected by poor lighting, extremes of temperature, or furniture arrangements? Is there a high concentration of carbon dioxide in the air? What is a good architectural environment in which to facilitate teaching and learning?

These questions can be used as the basis for a variety of interesting and challenging PBL lessons. Here is an example of a sequence of related PBL projects.

1. What does research say about effective architectural design to facilitate teaching and learning in a school? This question can be broken into a number of parts, with teams of students working on the various parts. Following are some examples of research topics for various teams.

   A. How much floor space is needed for each student in a classroom? Are there different space requirements for different ages of students? What furniture is needed, and what are good examples of furniture arrangements? What types of furniture and furniture arrangements can easily accommodate both didactic and constructivist instructional methods?

   B. How much light and what kind of light are appropriate? How can a classroom be designed to facilitate the use of media such as television, computer projection devices, and computers?

   C. What temperatures, air quality (for example, air pollution), and ventilation (airflow) are most appropriate in a classroom? How can one measure and monitor these variables?

   D. How should a classroom be designed to make it easy for students to hear each other and the teacher, and to see visual media presentations and the teacher?

   E. What are the special needs of students and staff who are physically challenged? Of course, access to the school building and classrooms is one consideration. But there are also issues such as access to science laboratory equipment and computers. The layout of furniture in a classroom may need to be adjusted to fit the needs of a wheelchair-bound student or a blind student.

   F. What about safety considerations? Possible safety threats include fire, chemicals (in a science lab), students pushing and shoving in the hallways and on stairways, and very bad weather.

   G. What about aesthetic considerations? Are teaching and learning affected by wall color, interior decorations, the appearance of the building, and plants or shrubbery within and outside the building?

   H. For each of the preceding points, what are the city, state, and federal building codes and other legal considerations or requirements? What is the history of these codes and legal considerations?

2. After the preceding projects are completed, additional projects that address other questions can be carried out. These issues include the following:

   A. How well does your classroom, school, other schools in your school district, or other schools in your state measure up to the legal and "desirable" standards identified in Item 1?

   B. Are there significant differences among cities, states, or countries in terms of the answers to Item 1?

   C. What can students do to improve the architectural environment of their classroom and school? Who can they enlist to help them? What are sources of resources?

   D. How can students share what they learn so that it will help other students in other schools, school districts, states, and nations?

The same general approach can be used to study the architectural environment of other buildings or of an entire city. Architecture is an interdisciplinary subject. Notice also that these questions regarding architectural environment can be used at a variety of grade levels and in different subject areas. Some of the students engaged in this type of project may decide that they want to seek further education in architecture and pursue a career in that field.

The Natural Environment

The natural environment provides many interesting and challenging projects that frequently focus on a local, regional, national, or international problem. Teams of students can work on a local problem, including teams from different classes in the school and teams from different schools. Teams from diverse locations can work on statewide, national, and global problems.

The Web site of the National Geographic Society (**www.nationalgeographic.com**) offers a wide range of material on the natural environment. It provides a good example of a commercial site that has a lot of content of interest to students and teachers.

Water is a natural resource that can be the basis for a variety of IT-assisted PBL lessons. A particular location may have too much water (floods) or too little water (drought). The water may be polluted. There may be conflicting demands placed on water use, such as recreation, agriculture, and manufacturing.

Air quality is another problem area that can be the basis for IT-assisted PBL lessons. Air pollution may be local, for example, in a valley, where air inversions trap automobile exhaust fumes. What are the levels of carbon monoxide, carbon dioxide, and other pollutants in your school or on your school grounds? Depletion of the ozone layer is a global problem.

Weather and weather forecasting can also be used in a wide range of IT-assisted PBL projects. Weather forecasting is a high-tech field that makes extensive use of IT. How do we know about weather from tens of thousands of years ago, before written records were being kept? What evidence do we have of global warming? What might be causing global warming, and what can we do about it?

PBL projects based on problems related to the natural environment tend to have many characteristics in common. Here are some questions to ask at the beginning of this type of project:

1. What is the problem? What is the current situation? What is the desirable situation? How long has the problem existed? What are the consequences of not solving the problem? (See Appendix B, "An Overview of Problem Solving," for further discussion of these problem-solving ideas.)

2. Is the problem purely local, or does it impact people and the environment over a relatively large area? Are the people being affected causing the problem or are they simply living in the same area as the people causing the problem? Acid rain can be caused by pollution-producing factories that are located hundreds of miles away.

3. What is the purpose of doing the project? Will it lead to action that will help solve the problem? Will it lead to a report and a call for action? Who is the intended audience? Who can take direct actions that will help solve the problem?

4. Why does the problem exist? What are the factors helping to create the problem? What are the factors preventing the solution to the problem? What resources would be needed to solve the problem? Who would be helped and who would be hurt by solving the problem?

These types of questions suggest that such projects require a substantial amount of research. Part of the research can be done through examination of historical and current records. Some of it can also be done by interviewing people and representatives of companies. Part of the research may require the gathering of empirical data.

Here are some common aspects of conducting empirical research:

1. What is the purpose of the research? What hypotheses are being tested? What is the nature and amount of quantitative and qualitative data needed to adequately test the hypotheses? Is the research instrument or methodology valid and reliable? Are the results of the research generalizable?

2. What descriptive data will be gathered? How will still and video cameras be used? How will field notes be recorded and processed?

3. Precisely what quantitative measurements will be made and where, when, and how will they be made? What instrumentation will be used? (The what, where, when, and how must be stated precisely so that others can understand and repeat the experiment.)

4. What will be done to ensure accuracy in both qualitative and quantitative data gathering and storage? Will the data be automatically stored in a computer or will it be transferred to a computer? Will it be recorded by hand? How will errors be detected and corrected in each of these cases? What provisions will be taken to ensure that data is not lost?

5. How will the data be analyzed? What provisions for gathering more data will be made if the analysis suggests that the data needs to be gathered again or more data is needed?

6. How will the results be reported? How will they be used in the product, presentation, or performance developed for the project?

Field research is difficult and time consuming. When done as part of a comprehensive project, it can help students learn a great deal about how people "do" science. Notice that the focus is on learning and doing science. The process may involve the use of a wide range of scientific instruments as well as IT. Indeed, modern science is highly dependent on IT and on the IT built into scientific instruments. However, the focus of the project remains on learning and doing science.

Physical Fitness

How physically fit is each member of the class? What is the average (mean, medium, mode) physical fitness of the class? How does the physical fitness change over the course of the year?

This project begins with the whole class working together to decide on measurable characteristics of physical fitness. This may require breaking the class into teams, with each team doing research and some experimentation on some individual components of physical fitness.

After the class agrees on the measures they want to use for physical fitness, the next step is to collect data on individuals and the whole class. After that, it is a "natural" to have individual students and the whole class set goals of improving their physical fitness over a period of months. IT can be used to store data and develop charts and graphs.

History

Chapter 1 described an IT-assisted PBL historical newspaper lesson that illustrates a history-based lesson. There are a number of other PBL projects that can be developed using history as a basis for the lesson.

To begin, let's go back to one of the first principles in designing curriculum. Every subject matter (every curriculum area) can be organized on the basis of the main (central, big, seminal, unifying) ideas. Identification of the big ideas is a good starting point for the development of a lesson plan on a particular curriculum topic. Once you have a good understanding of the big ideas and the big subideas in a specific curriculum area, you can then begin to think about which methods in your teaching repertoire might best help students learn the curriculum area.

Historians develop their understanding of history by pursuing many different big ideas. For example, economics (business, trade, trade routes) provides a way of looking at history. Social units and social organizations (family, community, schools) provide a way to look at history. Dynamic leadership (individuals with unusually powerful leadership characteristics) provides a way to look at history. Big events (for example, the large increase in the number of women working in factories that occurred during World War II in the United States) provide a way of studying history. New technology, such as the development of the steam engine and the electric motor can be a focus of study. And, of course, historians study the history of the development, implementation, and consequences of the big ideas in all fields.

It is easy to see that history is a relevant component of every discipline taught in schools, as well as an important subject area in its own right. Think about some nonhistory discipline you teach. Identify one of the big ideas in that discipline. Then think about the history of that big idea, and how the big idea changed the discipline and/or the world. You now have the basis for an interdisciplinary project!

For example, in biology courses and health courses students learn about germs. Aha! A big idea. How has medicine been affected by our steadily increasing knowledge of microorganisms that cause disease? What were the major historical developments? How have vaccines changed the world? Do all children throughout the world get vaccinations?

History projects require careful research based on multiple sources of information. If recent history is being studied, interviews with participants or others who were alive at the time provide important information. Photographs, audio recordings, and video recordings may be available. Historical documents and artifacts from the specific time period may bring a perspective that is quite different from what one finds in books and articles written years after the events.

A historical project might culminate in a written document, an electronic multimedia document, a performance, or a presentation. Each can be an excellent way to share one's findings and analysis.

Many teachers make the mistake of having a history-based PBL lesson focus mainly on the use of IT rather than on the history being studied. For example, a history or social studies teacher might give the following assignment: Create a hypermedia stack that contains at least eight cards and is about the development and initial use of vaccines to prevent disease. This is an assignment about creating an interactive multimedia stack—it is not a history assignment.

Contrast this with an assignment having a focus on historical research based on multiple sources of information and multiple perspectives. When doing this assignment, students learn to learn history, and they learn to do history research. They learn that the results of historical research can be presented in a number of different ways. One form of presentation is an interactive multimedia stack. This form of presentation has strengths and weaknesses relative to the large number of other available forms of presentation. When deciding on the specific form of presentation to use for a historical study, one should take into consideration the intended audience and the intended purpose of the study.

Math

A number of math educators support the idea of using a constructivist approach to math education. The standards developed by the National Council of Teachers of Mathematics place a major emphasis on having students generate and test hypotheses, do math explorations, and learn to solve a wide range of problems using mathematics as a tool.

IT brings new dimensions to math education. Here are four examples:

1. The Logo programming language and its spin-offs, such as MicroWorlds software from Logo Computer Systems, Incorporated (http://www.microworlds.com/). These resources provide exciting and challenging environments for exploring mathematics and other topics (Papert, 1993).

2. Powerful mathematics problem-solving tools. These tools can solve many of the types of problems that students currently learn to solve by hand. For example, handheld calculators can now solve single-variable equations and systems of linear equations, graph functions, differentiate functions, and integrate functions.

3. Computer-based systems. These systems have even more capabilities and are far more user friendly than calculators. For example, there is a variety of geometry programs that make it easy for students to test the geometry hypotheses they have generated.

4. Student-developed material. These resources can help the students themselves and others learn math. For example, students can develop and desktop publish a book, or they can develop computer-based interactive instructional materials.

One of the big ideas in mathematics is that most of the math taught in schools is rooted in historical attempts to find solutions to important problems people face. For example, geometry and trigonometry are rooted in measuring the earth, surveying, map making, and keeping track of one's location during an ocean voyage. This suggests that for any particular math topic being studied, the following two questions can be asked:

1. What good is it? (Variations on this question include "Why is this useful?" and "Why do I have to learn this?")

2. What role can calculators, computers, and other IT play in this topic?

The first question is critical to constructivist-based teaching and motivation. Students build on their current knowledge. Different students form different answers to the question "What good is it?" Much of the motivation for learning is internal, or intrinsic. If a student is unable to develop internally satisfying answers to the question "What good is it?," learning will be severely hampered. While a teacher can talk about the possible value of a particular topic in mathematics, the teacher's answer will often be different from the answers students develop for themselves.

The second question is important because mathematics and IT are inextricably intertwined. Each is a source of problems for the other, and each is an aid to solving the problems in the other. That is why college students majoring in computers and information science are required to take a lot of mathematics coursework.

The preceding two questions can serve as the basis for a year-long project in which students work together to produce a document (print or electronic) that answers the questions. The intended audience may be the students themselves as well as students who will take the course in the future.

Important Scientific Discoveries

What is the most important scientific discovery that people have made, and why? This project might begin with a whole-class discussion of science, science research, and the impact that science has had on the societies of our world.

Then the class can be divided into teams. Each team selects what it considers to be the most important scientific discovery that has ever been made. Team members do research on this discovery and the impact it has had on the societies of the world. They develop a written and/or an oral report.

Note that it may happen that two teams want to use the same scientific discovery. As the teacher, you may want to allow this, or you may want to forbid it.

A variation of this project is to specify a range of dates, such as discoveries before 1600, discoveries from 1600 to 1700, or other dates. This specification of a range of dates allows the project to be assigned a number of times during a school year, with different dates each time.

Another variation is to restrict the discoveries to a particular field, such as health and medicine, music, art and architecture, and so on.

Publication

The examples given thus far have been discipline oriented. The remaining examples in this chapter focus on IT tools. A project might focus on specific tools, or specific tools might be one of the focuses in a non-IT curriculum area.

Here are two big ideas in the publication world:

1. Computers and other IT facilitated the development of the desktop-publication industry. Students of all ages can learn about the design, development, and production of hardcopy documents.

2. Computers and other IT have facilitated the development of interactive electronic documents. Again, students of all ages can learn about the design, development, and production of interactive electronic documents.

It is important to recognize that both the desktop publication of hardcopy materials and the electronic publication of interactive materials are complex and large fields of study. Many people make a living through their expertise in these fields. There are hundreds of books and an extensive research literature to support these endeavors. A good summary of key ideas is given in Yoder and Smith (1995).

The complexity of the desktop-publication and interactive electronic publication fields creates a major challenge for teachers. Students enjoy having access to the power (the adult tools) for desktop publication and interactive electronic publication. They are quite willing to learn by doing, to learn by trial and error, to learn from each other. They are not bothered by the fact that the teacher does not know all about these exciting, rapidly changing areas.

But what is the role of the teacher? How does the teacher develop lessons, provide feedback, help students learn, and assess student learning when he or she has quite limited knowledge and skills in these areas? These questions are addressed in more detail in Chapter 7, which covers assessment. Keep in mind, however, that one of the goals in an IT-assisted PBL lesson is to create an environment in which the teacher will learn. You can still develop lessons where the major focus is on the subject matter content area (the non-IT curriculum), where you have a high level of experience and expertise, but make it clear to the students that they and you are learning together—that this is a unique opportunity for everyone to work together in a community of learners.

Slideshow

Students of all grade levels can learn to use a still digital camera, load pictures into a computer, and develop a slideshow. Similarly, they can learn to use a scanner and clip art. Here are some examples of slideshow projects.

All students select a topic that interests them and that they would like their fellow students to know more about. The project is to develop and present a slideshow on the topic. The visual materials might come from photographs (taken using a digital camera), scanned images, images created in paint or draw software, images from clip art collections, and so on.

The elementary school class is divided into teams. Each team is assigned a time block from the typical day's schedule. Blocks might include various subject areas as well as lunch, recess, and so on. Each team is to develop and do a slideshow-based presentation on their time block. All team members on the team should contribute to both the development and presentation components of their project.

Projects Based on Digital Communication

The Internet is a worldwide digital communications system. E-mail and the Web have become everyday tools used by many millions of people. Students from throughout the world can interact with each other and with a rapidly growing collection of data available on the Web.

E-mail is inexpensive and relatively reliable, making it possible to carry out collaborative projects with participants from throughout a country or the world. The possibilities seem limitless. Here are two major categories of such projects:

1. Projects addressing worldwide problems, where data from throughout the world is useful in addressing the problem. Air pollution, water pollution, and other types

of environmental problems fall into this category. These are challenging problems. How does one define the data to be gathered (the measurements to be made) so that young researchers throughout the world can share it? Good examples can be found on the TERC Web site at **www.terc.edu/**.

2. Projects that focus on making comparisons among different locations. For example, what does it cost to feed a family of four? Does this vary in different parts of a country or different parts of the world? What does it mean to "feed a family of four"? Does this vary with the average standard of living in different parts of the world?

E-mail-based projects can have a variety of goals, including these:

- To conduct original research. With some careful planning, it is possible for school-age children throughout the world to gather data that can be used to make original contributions to scientific knowledge.

- To learn about what life is like in other parts of the world. What is the same, and what is different? How are schools alike, and how do they differ? How is entertainment alike, and how does it differ? There are innumerable types of questions that can be explored. Students broaden their horizons and world views as they learn about their fellow students from other countries.

- To practice communication skills. It is a challenge to communicate with people who have different cultures and experiences, even when their native language is the same. If one or both communicants are just learning to use a language, this presents another major challenge. Is the available language translation software really useful?

Web Search Engines

One of the goals of education is to help students learn to find information on a wide variety of topics. The Web can be thought of as a Global Digital Library. It is very large and is growing quite rapidly.

A Web search engine is a piece of software designed to help a person search for information on the Web. There are a large number of different search engines (**http://searchenginewatch.com**). Here several different ideas for PBL lessons related to search engines.

1. Each team of students is assigned a different search engine. The team is to do a project that explores the capabilities and limitations, the advantages and disadvantages, of possible use of this search by students at their grade level.

2. Each team of students is assigned a different search engine. The team is to develop a users manual suitable for use by their peers.

3. The class as a whole is to undertake the project of determine the "best" search engine for use by the class.

4. Each team is to be assigned a discipline area, such as art, language arts, math, music, science, social studies, and so on. Each team is to attempt to find a search engine that is especially good for doing searches within their specific discipline area. They are to develop and present evidence of why the search engine they select is especially good in their specific discipline.

Projects Based on Generic Software Tools

There are a number of software tools now considered to be "generic," or general purpose. Examples include word processors, databases, spreadsheets, paint and draw graphics tools, hypermedia, e-mail, and Web browsers.

The International Society for Technology in Education (ISTE) (1998) has developed a set of National Educational Technology Standards for IT in K–12 education, which is available on the ISTE Web site (**www.iste.org**). These standards include a focus on having students learn to use the generic tools and then using the tools as they are integrated throughout the everyday curriculum.

Under these standards, the expectation is that students will develop a reasonable level of functionality in using a wide range of generic tools by the time they finish the sixth or seventh grade. As such standards become widely accepted and implemented, teachers at the 8–12 grade level will be able to assume that their students are facile in using the generic tools.

This means, for example, that for any topic a teacher is teaching, students can be asked to do projects that explore the roles of the generic tools in solving the problems and communicating the results. To take a specific example, consider the set of graphing tools in a modern spreadsheet program. Study and research in many different subjects requires the gathering, analysis, and representation of data. Data might be represented by a pie chart, a bar graph, a line graph, a scatter plot, and so forth. One question to pose is: What form of graph best communicates a given type of data?

What are students in schools in other cities, states, and nations learning about the generic tools? How do the standards being developed in the United States (or in specific states) compare with the standards being developed in other countries? How can one compare the knowledge and skills that students in widely scattered locations are gaining? These questions can be the basis for interesting and challenging projects.

Projects Based on Domain-Specific Tools

Any academic discipline can be analyzed from the point of view of the problems it addresses and methodologies used to solve these problems. Every teacher teaches problem solving. Computers and other IT tools are an aid to problem solving.

Appendix B, "An Overview of Problem Solving," provides a general discussion of problem solving. One of the most important ideas in problem solving is that knowledge is built on your own previous work and on the previous work of others. Nowadays, the knowledge and skills may be embodied in IT hardware and software and in the rapidly growing Global Digital Library.

The preceding section of this chapter discussed generic computer tools. In addition to generic tools, there are special purpose computer tools that have been developed in each academic area. These are often called domain-specific tools. Within any course, students can work individually and collectively to identify these tools, learn about their uses and how to use the tools themselves, and study the impact the tools are having on the discipline covered in the course. The professional IT tools of an artist are quite different from those of a musician or an engineer.

Here is a word of warning. If you assign such a project, be prepared to deal with the fact that students may discover that part of what you are teaching is now out of date and may be irrelevant because of progress in IT. For example, graphing calculators and computers with graphing software are very accurate and fast at graphing functions. What level of by-hand graphing skills should students be expected to gain in a math course? Or consider the effects of computer-assisted design. This computer capability has almost completely replaced the types of skills that used to be taught in mechanical drawing courses in high schools and technical schools.

Another example is provided by the IT hardware and software developed by the music industry. Much music is created, stored, edited, and performed using this hardware and software. This has transformed the music industry. Even elementary school students can learn to use these tools. They can compose music either as a goal in its own right or as a component of a larger project.

Electronic Portfolio

The development and presentation of a portfolio of one's work is a good ongoing project. One of the key ideas in a portfolio is that one collects and analyzes much more material than will be used in one specific presentation. The material in a portfolio may consist of hardcopy, audiotapes, videotapes, and other formats. Now, it is becoming common to digitize one's portfolio items and store them on computer media. The result is called an electronic portfolio. This makes it easy to edit the material, add annotations to the material, and to select components to be used in a particular presentation of one's work.

Final Remarks

IT-assisted PBL lessons can be developed in every academic area. The future envisioned by this book is one in which IT becomes ubiquitous—it will be available everywhere. (Chapter 8 discusses the future of IT in education.) IT will become a routinely used, everyday tool at work, at play, and at school. Interactivity, new communication systems, the Global Digital Library, and other IT-assisted aids to problem solving will also be used routinely. IT-assisted PBL provides an instructional environment that can help prepare students for this future world of ubiquitous computers.

Activities

1. The Global Schoolhouse Web site (**www.gsn.org**) includes a substantial focus on PBL. Explore this site and report on what you find. Analyze the usefulness of the list of projects on the site at **www.gsn.org/pr/**.

2. Pick a subject matter that interests you. Name one or more current important problems or issues the subject matter addresses. Do a Web search in which you look for information that relates to these problems and issues. Analyze the information you find for possible use in an IT-based PBL lesson.

3. The U.S. government maintains a large number of Web sites designed for use by students and teachers (**www.ed.gov/free/subject.html**). Find a topic area that you feel is appropriate for the students you teach and briefly describe a PBL lesson on that topic.

the case for PBL

PBL is a versatile approach to instruction that can readily be used in conjunction with other approaches. A huge number of articles have been written about PBL. Most, however, are specific examples and testimonials rather than carefully conducted research studies.

This chapter discusses a number of different types of arguments that support the use of PBL and IT-assisted PBL in the classroom. In total, they present a strong case for increased use of PBL in K–12 education.

Research Areas Supporting PBL

This section contains very brief summaries of some of the areas of educational research that underlie PBL.

Constructivism

It is now well understood that each student brings a unique set of knowledge, skills, and experiences to a new learning situation. Constructivism is a widely supported educational theory that rests on the idea that students create their own knowledge in the context of their own experiences (Fosnot, 1996). Constructivism focuses on students being actively engaged in doing rather than passively engaged in receiving knowledge. PBL can be viewed as one approach to creating learning environments in which students construct personal knowledge.

Willis and Mehlinger (1996) provide an excellent discussion of three different forms of constructivism and their roles in teacher education. Cognitive, social, and political constructivism lead to somewhat different approaches to instruction; but all differ substantially from a didactic (behavioral) approach. Willis and Mehlinger indicate that constructivism is rapidly growing in acceptance.

The President's Committee of Advisors on Science and Technology (1997) offers a careful analysis of the constructivist literature, especially as it relates to IT in education. The committee finds the case for constructivism to be compelling but cautions that there is substantial need for additional research. The report recommends that constructivism be the underlying theory guiding implementation of IT in education.

For five years Seymour Papert (1980, 1993) studied under Piaget at a postdoctoral level. The Logo programming language Papert later helped develop was designed to create a computer-based constructivist learning environment. There is a huge amount of research literature on the use of Logo in education. In brief, the literature suggests that the tool (Logo and the environments created from it) does not automatically guarantee educational success. The knowledge and skills of the teacher facilitating this learning environment tend to be the most powerful predictors of student success.

The research on Logo conveys an important message. While IT-assisted PBL is an excellent vehicle for implementing a constructivist theory of teaching and learning, a significant contributor to student success is the teacher's knowledge and skills.

Situated Learning

Lave and Wegner (1991) argue that a key aspect of a learning activity is the context and culture in which it occurs. As they discuss situated learning, they argue that most classroom learning activities are abstract and out of context. This lessens the quality of learning and transfer of learning.

Consistent with research in social constructivist learning theory, Lave and Wegner argue that social interaction is a critical component of learning. In appropriately designed situated learning, learners become involved in a "community of practice" that embodies certain beliefs and behaviors to be acquired. One of the goals in the design and implementation of a PBL lesson is to achieve this community of practice situation in which both students and the teacher are actively engaged in carrying out a project.

A number of researchers have explored situated learning and are supportive of it. A variation of situated learning is called anchored instruction. The Jasper Woodbury materials developed at Vanderbilt University provide an excellent example use of situated learning (anchored instruction) in the design of instructional materials (**http://peabody.vanderbilt.edu/projects/funded/jasper/**). In the Jasper Woodbury adventures, students learn by solving problems that are situated in interesting and somewhat authentic environments.

Motivation Theory

In an article that is part of the ongoing PBL research and implementation at the University of Michigan, Blumenfeld et al. (1991) provide an extensive review of the research literature supporting PBL. For many years, Elliot Soloway, one of the coauthors of the Blumenfeld et al. article, has been heading up projects exploring the use of computers and other IT in PBL.

The article presents two major arguments for using PBL: It enhances motivation and fosters cognitive engagement. The research literature supporting these two benefits is strong. In essence, it says that if students are motivated and cognitively engaged, they will learn more and remember it better, as compared to learning through didactic instruction or carrying out projects they do not find motivating.

The article also notes that it is not easy to develop and teach PBL lessons that students will find motivating and cognitively engaging. It suggests a number of ideas to increase the likelihood of success, including making the problems being addressed relevant to students and having them play a major role both in selecting specific projects and deciding how to conduct their related work. Staff development is a major factor in helping teachers learn to create successful IT-assisted PBL environments.

Inquiry-Based Learning

Teachers using PBL often use inquiry-based teaching methods. Inquiry-based learning, or discovery-based learning, is a common tool in science education. In essence, it is an approach to help students learn about hypothesis generation and testing—the scientific method. The emphasis may be on discovering specific facts or on developing a higher-order understanding of the topic and ideas being explored. In either case, students are encouraged to develop curiosity as a habit of mind and to approach all learning with a disposition toward questioning and systematic investigation.

Research indicates that hands-on, inquiry-based instruction is generally more effective than traditional didactic presentation in improving problem-solving ability in particular subject domains (Helgeson, 1992).

Math education has also moved in the direction of inquiry-based learning. Math educators use the terminology "problem posing" rather than "hypothesis generation." Students learn to search for patterns, develop hypotheses about the patterns, and then test (prove) the hypotheses. Problem solving is a major theme in mathematics education and in every other academic discipline. (Appendix B, "An Overview of Problem Solving," provides more information about problem solving.)

Cooperative Learning

Teachers using IT-assisted PBL frequently use teams of students who address a complex problem or task. Typically, each student has individual learning and product development responsibilities, and the whole group has group goals. Peer instruction is a common and expected component of this learning environment. PBL provides an authentic environment in which teachers can help students increase their cooperative-learning skills.

Cooperative learning has been extensively researched. In a typical cooperative-learning environment, class members are grouped into teams of three to four students who work together to explore and learn a curriculum topic. Sometimes the learning task is split into pieces, with each student being responsible for mastering one component and then helping others in the team learn about that component.

Cooperative learning has been shown to be effective in improving academic and social skills; however, successful cooperative learning requires careful organization and sometimes explicit training in collaboration and communication (Johnson, 1986; Johnson & Johnson, 1989).

Problem Solving and Collaborative Problem Solving

In IT-assisted PBL, students focus on a challenging problem or task. There has been substantial research on teaching problem solving and improving students' higher-order thinking skills (Moursund, 2001; Perkins, 1992, 1995). A summary of key ideas about teaching problem solving is given in Appendix B, "An Overview of Problem Solving." In general, students can get better at solving complex problems and accomplishing complex tasks through practice and explicit instruction. The practice needs to be in an environment that presents challenging problems and tasks. Students need to be intrinsically motivated.

All these conditions can be satisfied in a PBL environment facilitated by a teacher who has good knowledge about key ideas in problem solving.

Research on problem solving indicates that in many cases, two heads are better than one. This has led to the development of a category of software called groupware. Groupware is designed to facilitate two or more people who need not be located in the same place to work together on a problem or task.

With groupware, people at remote locations can view the same screen, communicate with each other, and contribute individually to making changes on the computer screen. This facilitates collaborative work.

Up until now, relatively few schools have made groupware available to their students. However, many schools have facilitated their students engaging in PBL with other students located at remote sites. Eventually it will become commonplace for students to use groupware and to collaborate with students located at other sites.

Problem-Based Learning

Problem-based learning can be considered as a type of PBL where students focus on a problem that has been specified for them. This problem may be quite specific, as a medical, business, or social problem. The problem often has some or all of the following characteristics:

- It is messy, complex, and often ill defined
- It requires inquiry, information gathering, and higher-order thinking
- It has no simple, fixed, formulaic, "right" solution

In some cases, students throughout the country address the same problem. Regional and national contests identify winners, who are awarded prizes. For example, the problem might be to build a solar-powered model car, or to build a bridge out of balsa wood that reaches across a two-foot span and can support a heavy load. In both cases, there are carefully stated restrictions on the resources that can be used in solving the problem. In the bridge-building problem, for example, only a specified amount of balsa wood, glue, and string might be available.

Problem-based learning is commonly used in such diverse areas as architecture education, business education, and medical education. This suggests that problem-based learning has proven effective in a variety of teaching/learning settings.

An ERIC search on problem-based learning identifies a significant number of documents. However, most of these documents are case studies or testimonials. Overall, those who write these articles tend to be quite supportive of problem-based learning. They describe the enthusiasm of teams of students putting in long hours on their projects. They describe the thrill of victory, the agony of defeat, and the fun that students have while working on such problems. Glasgow (1997) provides an excellent overview of problem-based learning from a secondary teacher's point of view. Glasgow's book provides an extended analysis of and testimonial on the use of problem-based learning in education.

Other Arguments Supporting PBL

This section explores some arguments for IT-assisted PBL based on the observation that it is aligned with a variety of generally accepted educational goals.

Learning to Carry Out Interdisciplinary Projects

PBL is an excellent vehicle for helping students learn to work together to carry out complex interdisciplinary projects. Goldman's (1995) work on emotional intelligence provides good insights into the emotional characteristics that support people being successful in working individually and in teams to carry out complex tasks.

Learning how to carry out complex interdisciplinary projects is an explicit educational goal in many school systems. Indeed, some colleges organize their curriculum along interdisciplinary lines. The reasoning behind this is that real-world problems are almost always interdisciplinary. Thus, students should learn to work in interdisciplinary environments.

One of the challenges of interdisciplinary problems is that often a single person lacks the knowledge, skills, and time needed to solve the problem. It takes a team of experts whose members represent the various disciplines to address the problem in a timely manner. This team approach to problem solving is common in the world of business and industry.

It is not easy to learn to work in a collaborative team environment. How does a team member provide constructive feedback to other team members without antagonizing them? How can the overall task be divided into equitable pieces? How does the team deal with team members who do not carry their weight? How are disputes resolved?

The interdisciplinary nature of most IT-assisted PBL lessons is a challenge to students whose education has been highly compartmentalized. In our traditional compartmentalized educational system, students often experience trouble in transferring knowledge from one subject area domain to solving a problem in another domain. For example, students may learn about the metric system in a math class and then be unable to apply this knowledge in a science class. PBL provides an excellent environment for working on transfer of learning. More information about transfer of learning is given in Appendix B, "An Overview of Problem Solving."

Focusing on Higher-Order Thinking Skills

One of the defining characteristics of PBL is a focus on students addressing challenging problems and tasks and improving their higher-order thinking skills. Perkins (1992) summarizes the research literature in support of emphasizing higher-order skills. He argues that students who learn their lower-order knowledge and skills in a higher-order skills environment will retain them better than students who are taught in an environment that specifically focuses on lower-order knowledge and skills.

Perkins' work contains an excellent overview of education and the wide variety of attempts to improve our educational system. He analyzes these attempted improvements in terms of how well they contribute to accomplishing three major goals of education:

1. Acquisition and retention of knowledge and skills.

2. Understanding of one's acquired knowledge and skills.

3. Active use of one's acquired knowledge and skills (the ability to apply one's learning to new settings and the ability to analyze and solve novel problems).

In some sense, these three goals form a continuum from lower-order to middle-order to higher-order knowledge and skills. Every educational system faces the problem of deciding how much emphasis to place on lower-order versus middle-order versus higher-order knowledge and skills. It often happens that a particular educational system tends to cycle its emphasis over a period of years. There will be a back-to-basics movement, followed by a major emphasis on helping students to improve their higher-order cognitive processes, and then another back-to-basics movement. The current emphasis of the federal government in the United States on national and state testing has many characteristics of a back-to-basics movement.

While the back-to-basics movement remains strong throughout the world, there is increasing research evidence that supports the contention that a good education requires a substantial emphasis on higher-order knowledge and skills. This presents educators with the task of developing curriculum, instruction, and assessment that is appropriately balanced between lower-order and higher-order knowledge and skills.

Parallels with Process Writing

Process writing has been thoroughly researched and widely implemented (Boone, 1991). Many teachers—even those who do not teach writing—are familiar with writing as a process. The six steps of process writing are:

1. Brainstorming

2. Organizing the brainstormed ideas

3. Developing a draft

4. Obtaining feedback

5. Revising

6. Publishing

One of the most important ideas in writing is summarized by the statement "revise, revise, revise." Computers have proven to be a useful tool in process writing. Computers are especially useful in the revision stage of process writing.

One can draw a parallel between PBL and process writing. Of course, a PBL lesson often requires writing. But one can also consider the process of carrying out a project. The steps of process writing are similar to the steps used to carry out a project. The basic nature of producing a product, presentation, or performance is supportive of a "revise, revise, revise" approach.

Communication and Other Goals for IT in Education

Many states have explicit goals for IT in education, or they have incorporated such goals within the goals for the non-IT curriculum domains. The International Society for Technology in Education (ISTE) (1998) has developed National Educational Technology Standards for students at the preK–12 level. Appendix A provides a summary of this document, which is also available in complete form on the ISTE Web site at **www.iste.org**.

Communication is a recurring theme in the various state standards and in the ISTE standards. Students need to gain skills in communication both in a print (hardcopy) environment and in an interactive digital environment. Thus, both desktop publication and desktop presentation (using a projection system or other display process) are important.

Some schools have developed explicit courses for writing in a desktop-publication environment and for developing effective hypermedia stacks and Web pages. IT specialists may teach such courses, perhaps with students going to a computer lab to receive the instruction.

The trend, however, is for such instruction to occur in the "regular" classroom, where it is taught by the regular classroom teacher. This helps the instruction to be more aligned with the rest of the curriculum. IT-assisted PBL can be an excellent vehicle to support such instruction. Moreover, this environment usually requires teams of students to work together on a complex project. As noted previously, learning to work in a team environment is an important goal in education.

The typical classroom teacher has had little formal instruction and practice in desktop publication or in the development of interactive hypermedia documents. While staff development is sorely needed, other approaches are also essential. IT-assisted PBL creates an environment in which teachers can learn alongside their students.

Learning to Use Your Intelligence

This section contains arguments for PBL based on research into human intelligence. The general flavor of the arguments is that we want students to develop their higher-order thinking and problem-solving skills. We want them to learn to use their brains effectively. PBL can be used to create learning environments that will help students learn to use their brains more effectively.

Solving problems and carrying out complex tasks requires having the necessary resources available and then using these resources effectively. One resource all individuals have is their own intelligence that is incorporated in their mind and body. Actually, it is much more accurate to speak of one's intelligences. Each person has varying levels of intelligence in different areas. For example, a person may have a high level of musical intelligence but a relatively low level of logical/mathematical intelligence.

Howard Gardner, Robert Sternberg, and David Perkins are three researchers and writers who have made significant contributions to our understanding of intelligence; some of their ideas are covered in this section. This section also poses a definition of intelligence and then explores a variety of intelligences that people have. Effective PBL helps students develop and use their various intelligences.

A Definition of Intelligence

The study and measurement of intelligence has been an important research topic for nearly 100 years. IQ is a complex concept, and researchers in this field argue with each other about the various theories that have been developed. There is no clear agreement about what constitutes IQ or how to measure it. There is an extensive and continually growing collection of research papers on the topic. Howard Gardner (1983, 1993), Robert Sternberg (1988, 1997), and David Perkins (1995) have written widely sold books that summarize the literature and present their own points of view.

The following definition of intelligence is a composite from various authors, drawing especially on the work of Gardner, Perkins, and Sternberg. Intelligence is a combination of the abilities to:

1. Learn. This includes all kinds of informal and formal learning through any combination of experience, education, and training.

2. Pose problems. This includes recognizing problem situations and transforming them into more clearly defined problems.

3. Solve problems. This includes solving problems, accomplishing tasks, fashioning products, and doing complex projects.

This definition of intelligence is a very optimistic one. It says that each of us can become more intelligent. We can become more intelligent through study and practice, through access to appropriate tools, and through learning to use these tools effectively (Perkins, 1995).

PBL can be used as a vehicle in which students can use and improve their intelligence. More detail on the work of Gardner, Sternberg, and Perkins is given in the next three subsections.

Howard Gardner

Some researchers in the field of intelligence have long argued that people have a variety of different intelligences. A person may be good at learning languages and terrible at learning music—or vice versa. A single number (a score on an IQ test) cannot adequately represent the complex and diverse capabilities of a human being.

Howard Gardner (1993) has proposed a theory of multiple intelligences. He originally identified seven components of intelligence. He argues that these intelligences are relatively distinct from each other and that each person has some level of each of these seven intelligences. More recently, he has added an eighth intelligence to his list (Educational Leadership, 1997). Figure 4.1 describes these intelligences.

Many teachers who use PBL have studied the work of Howard Gardner and use some of his ideas in their teaching. For example, in creating a team of students to do a particular project, a teacher may select a team whose collective "highest" talents encompass most of the eight areas of intelligence Gardner identifies. The teacher may encourage a team to divide up specific tasks in line with specific high levels of talent found on a team. Alternatively, a teacher may encourage or require team members not to work in their areas of highest ability in order to encourage their development of knowledge and skills in other areas.

FIGURE 4.1

Gardner's eight intelligences and examples of each.

Intelligence	Examples	Discussion
Bodily-kinesthetic	Dancers, athletes, surgeons, crafts people	The ability to use one's physical body well.
Interpersonal	Sales people, teachers, clinicians, politicians, religious leaders	The ability to sense others' feelings and be in tune with others.
Intrapersonal	People who have good insight into themselves and use their other intelligences effectively	Self-awareness. The ability to know your own body and mind.
Linguistic	Poets, writers, orators, communicators	The ability to communicate well, perhaps both orally and in writing, perhaps in several languages.
Logical-mathematical	Mathematicians, logicians	The ability to learn higher mathematics. The ability to handle complex logical arguments.
Musical	Musicians, composers	The ability to learn, perform, and compose music.
Naturalistic	Biologists, naturalists	The ability to understand different species, recognize patterns in nature, classify natural objects.
Spatial	Sailors navigating without modern navigational aids, surgeons, sculptors, painters	The ability to know where you are relative to fixed locations. The ability to accomplish tasks requiring three-dimensional visualization and placement of your hands or other parts of your body.

Figure 4.1 lists the eight intelligences Gardner has identified. It provides some examples of the types of professionals who exhibit a high level of each intelligence. The eight intelligences are listed in alphabetical order.

At this point, you might want to do some introspection. For each of the eight intelligences in Gardner's list, think about your own level of talents and performance. For each intelligence, decide if you have an area of expertise that makes substantial use of the intelligence. For example, perhaps you are good at music. If so, is music the basis of your vocation?

Students can also do this type of introspection, and it can become a routine component of PBL lessons. Students can come to understand that they are more naturally gifted in some areas than in others, but that they have some talent in all of the eight areas. Curriculum and instruction can be developed to help all students make progress in enhancing their talents in each of these eight areas of intelligence.

Robert Sternberg

Many teachers have provided testimonial evidence that PBL encourages participation on the part of their students who have a high level of "street smarts" but who do not have a high level of "school smarts." They report that some of their students who were not doing well in school have become actively engaged and experienced a high level of success in working on projects. These observations are consistent with and supportive of the research of Robert Sternberg.

As noted previously in this chapter, different researchers have identified different components of intelligence. Sternberg (1988, 1997) focuses on just three main components:

1. Practical intelligence—the ability to do well in informal and formal educational settings, adapting to and shaping one's environment; street smarts.

2. Experiential intelligence—the ability to deal with novel situations, the ability to effectively automate ways of dealing with novel situations so that they are easily handled in the future, the ability to think in novel ways.

3. Componential intelligence—the ability to process information effectively. This includes metacognitive, executive, performance, and knowledge-acquisition components that help to steer cognitive processes.

Sternberg provides examples of people who are quite talented in one of these areas but not so talented in the other two. In that sense, his approach to the field of intelligence is somewhat like Gardner's. However, you can see that Sternberg does not focus on specific components of intelligence that are aligned with various academic disciplines. He is far more concerned with helping people develop components of intelligence that will help them perform well in whatever they choose to do.

Sternberg strongly believes that intelligence can be increased by study and practice. Quite a bit of his research focuses on such endeavors. Some of Sternberg's work focuses specifically on "street smarts" versus "school smarts." He notes that some people are particularly talented in one of these two areas but not in the other. This observation is consistent with the work of Lev Vygotsky (Fosnot, 1996), who argues that the type of learning that goes on outside of school is distinctly different from the type that goes on in school. While some students are talented in both informal and formal education, others are much more successful in one than in the other. A teacher who is skillful in developing PBL can help students design projects that are consistent with their learning abilities and interests.

David Perkins

In his book Smart Schools, David Perkins (1992) analyzes a number of different educational theories and approaches to education. His analysis is strongly supportive of Gardner's theory of multiple intelligences. (They have been professional colleagues for many years.) Perkins' book describes extensive research-based evidence showing that education can be considerably improved by more explicitly teaching for transfer, by focusing on higher-order cognitive skills, and by using PBL.

In another work, Perkins (1995) examines a large number of research studies both on the measurement of IQ and on programs of study designed to increase IQ. He presents detailed arguments that IQ has three major components or dimensions:

1. Neural intelligence. This refers to the efficiency and precision of one's neurological system.

2. Experiential intelligence. This refers to one's accumulated knowledge and experience in different areas. It can be thought of as the accumulation of all of the expertise one has gained.

3. Reflective intelligence. This refers to one's broad-based strategies for attacking problems, for learning, and for approaching intellectually challenging tasks. It includes attitudes that support persistence, systemization, and imagination. It includes self-monitoring and self-management.

There is substantial evidence to support the belief that a child's neural intelligence can be adversely affected by the mother's use of drugs such as alcohol and cocaine during pregnancy. Lead (for example, from lead-based paint) can do severe neural damage to a person. Vitamins, or the lack thereof, can also affect neural intelligence. An inadequate diet (starvation) adversely affects children's neural intelligence.

Moreover, there is general agreement that neural intelligence has a "use it or lose it" characteristic. It is clear that neural intelligence can be maintained and, indeed, increased, by use.

Experiential intelligence is based on years and years of accumulating knowledge and experience in both informal and formal learning environments. Such knowledge and experience can lead to a high level of expertise in one or more fields. People who live in "rich" learning environments have a significant intelligence advantage over people who grow up in less-stimulating environments. Experiential intelligence can be increased by such environments.

Reflexive intelligence can be thought of as a control system that helps one use neural intelligence and experiential intelligence effectively. In fact, a person can learn strategies that help him or her use neural intelligence and experiential intelligence more effectively. The habits of mind included under reflexive intelligence can be learned and improved. Metacognition and other approaches to reflecting about one's cognitive processes can also help.

Reasons for Using PBL

A search of the literature identifies a large number of articles on classroom projects. Most of these reports are testimonials—teachers explaining how they use projects in their teaching and giving their perceptions of how successful these projects have been. Benefits attributed to PBL include the following:

• Increased motivation. Accounts of projects often report that students willingly devote extra time or effort to the project or that previously hard-to-reach students begin to participate in class. Teachers often report improvements in attendance and decreases in tardiness. Students often report that projects are more fun and more engaging than other components of the curriculum.

- Increased problem-solving ability. Research on improving students' higher-order cognitive skills emphasizes the need for students to engage in problem-solving tasks and the need for specific instruction on how to attack and solve problems (Moursund, 2001; Perkins, 1992). Many articles describe PBL environments in which students become actively and successfully engaged in posing and solving complex problems.

- Improved library research skills. Most projects require students to move beyond readily available printed information sources such as textbooks, encyclopedias, and dictionaries. IT offers excellent additional sources of information, including those on CD-ROM and the Internet. The emphasis of PBL on independent research is in keeping with the American Library Association's call for information literacy as a fundamental goal. The association defines information literacy as the ability to know when there is a need for information, identify and find the needed information, evaluate and organize the information, and use the information effectively to address the problem or issue at hand (Breivik & Senn, 1994). PBL can provide an authentic and motivating context in which to gain increased information literacy.

- Increased collaboration. The necessity for group work in many projects requires students to develop and practice communication skills (Johnson & Johnson, 1989). Peer teaching, student evaluation, online information sharing, and cooperative learning groups are all aspects of the collaborative nature of projects. Current cognitive theories suggest that learning is a social phenomenon and that students will learn more in a collaborative environment (Wiburg & Carter, 1994).

- Increased resource-management skills. Part of becoming an independent learner involves taking responsibility for completing complex tasks. Well-implemented PBL gives students instruction and practice in organizing projects and in allocating time and other resources, such as equipment, to complete tasks on schedule.

Final Remarks

This chapter has briefly summarized many different types of arguments supporting the use of IT-assisted PBL in education. Education is a very complex field, and there are many different approaches to successful teaching and to helping students learn. The current state of educational research does not allow us to expect that researchers will produce unassailable evidence that one particular approach is superior to all others. However, the evidence presented in this chapter strongly suggests that IT-assisted PBL should be part of the teaching repertoire of most teachers.

Activities

1. Select an IT-assisted PBL lesson idea from Chapter 3. Analyze it from the point of view of Gardner, Perkins, and Sternberg in terms of how the lesson helps students use and improve their intelligences.

2. Make a list of arguments against increased use of IT-assisted PBL in your own teaching. Which of these arguments are countered by the ideas presented in this chapter?

3. Teachers often ask the question" How can I make more use of PBL at a time when my school administrators are demanding that I spend more time teaching to the tests that our students have to take?" Develop an answer to this question.

CHAPTER 5

project planning

If you don't know where you are going, you will probably end up somewhere else.

— *Laurence J. Peter (1912 – 1988)*

A project can be viewed as a problem to be solved or a task to be accomplished. Careful thinking and planning at the beginning—before starting to carry out the work required on specific components of the project—is essential. This chapter covers the rudiments of planning for carrying out a project. You need to think about these ideas as you develop a PBL lesson and monitor your students' work on projects. You also need to help your students learn these ideas.

Project Planning—Getting Started

What do your students know about doing projects, and what do they need to learn about doing a project? The chances are that your students vary widely in their previous experience in undertaking individual and group projects. Thus, a good starting point is to do a needs assessment to determine their background and experience in doing projects. For example, have your students talk about or write about fun and challenging projects they have done. Encourage them to write about the planning process, budgeting their time, and working with other students.

In getting started in IT-assisted PBL, many teachers make the mistake of expecting too much of their students. For example, consider this set of directions to a group of young students for a project called People Are the Same and Different:

> We are going to do a project on how people and life in other countries are alike and different from people and life in our country. Projects will be done by teams of two students. We will work on this project for two weeks. However, during the last three days, students will present reports and we will spend time discussing these reports.

1. Get together with a partner. Pick a foreign country that interests your team. Then pick at least two everyday parts of life in that country, such as what people eat, what clothes they wear, what jobs they have, what schools are like, what transportation is used, and so on. Turn in a one-paragraph report giving the names of the two people on your team, the name of the country, and the parts of life in the country you are going to study. This paragraph is due at the end of class tomorrow.

2. Do research using the school library, the Web, and other sources to find general information about the country and specific information about the parts of life in the country your team selected in Item 1.

3. Write a report that contains the information from Item 2. Your report should compare and contrast this information with our country.

4. The report you wrote for Item 3 is to be word processed and desktop published. It is due on [specified due date].

5. Each team will present a five-minute report to the whole class during the last three days of the project. A sign-up sheet will be posted in the back of the room tomorrow morning.

6. You will be graded on the quality of your research, the quality of the writing and content of your paper, the quality of your desktop publishing, the quality of your oral presentation, and getting the project done on time. Equal weight will be given to each of these five items.

Initially, most young students will have difficulty with this range of options and will not understand how to begin or to undertake such a project. They may not be familiar with many foreign countries. Perhaps none of the countries will interest them. They may have no idea that food, clothing, jobs, and schools are different in different countries. They may not know how to work with a partner on a two-person team.

If your students have difficulty making the initial decisions about what to study in a project, chances are that they will benefit from some whole-class didactic instruction on the overall topic area of the proposed project. For example, the students might do some worksheets that help them study some similarities and differences among countries. What are family life, home, school, work, play, stores, and so on like in different parts of our country and in different countries?

Alternatively, the whole class might work together on a short project. The teacher might assign each pair of students a country. A two-person team can find information about the country (location, land area, population, climate, and so forth) and life in the country (food, clothing, housing, jobs, education, and so on). Each team might give a short report to the class, and the teacher can lead a whole-class discussion on similarities and differences among countries. The goal is to build some common background for the students in the class.

Now look back at the project specifications for "People Are the Same and Different." Notice the assessment specifications in this project. Are your students familiar with multipart grading criteria? And what about the desktop-publication component of the project? Do your students understand what constitutes doing a good job of desktop publication?

Beginners need to gain an initial level of skill by working on relatively short and simple projects. These may be lockstep projects, with every student in the class doing essentially the same project, following the same timeline, and meeting the same milestones (intermediate requirements); however, even very young students can learn to take initiative, help define the scope and goals of their specific project, and take responsibility for meeting timelines.

Over a period of time, students can learn to carry out complex projects that require careful planning, allocation of resources, use of higher-order thinking skills, and persistence. But this level of success does not come easily. It is a goal that can be achieved through many years of instruction and experience.

Project Planning for Students and Teachers

A Project Planning Table like the one in Figure 5.1 can be particularly useful for beginners (both students and teachers). It represents a project as a sequence of tasks (with underlying subtasks) to be accomplished. This planning table includes a description of each task and subtask, the resources needed or available, a timeline, and milestones.

FIGURE 5.1

Project Planning Table.

	Description	Resources	Timeline	Milestones
Task 1				
Subtask 1.1				
Subtask 1.2				
Task 2				
Etc.				

The amount of detail one needs to give in a Project Planning Table varies with the students' knowledge and experience. Each component is discussed in the following sections.

Description of Tasks in Outline Form

Begin by developing an outline of the tasks to be accomplished. Here is an outline for the "People Are the Same and Different" project described in the previous section.

Task 1: Get started.

   1.1 Select a partner.

   1.2 Select a country.

   1.3 Select two or more parts of everyday life in the country.

   1.4 Prepare and turn in a one-paragraph report summarizing 1.1 to 1.3.

Task 2: Do research.

   2.1 Use the CD-ROM encyclopedia available in our classroom.

   2.2 Use the Web.

   2.3 Use books and magazines in our school library.

Task 3: Write a first draft of a comparison/contrast report using a word processor.

Task 4: Polish and publish the report.

    4.1 Edit and revise the report.

    4.2 Desktop publish the report.

    4.3 Turn in the report on the date due.

Task 5: Make an oral presentation.

    5.1 Prepare an oral report and accompanying desktop-published presentation materials.

    5.2 Rehearse the oral report and revise as needed.

    5.3 Present the oral report.

There is a strong parallel between developing a Project Planning Table and the ideas presented in Appendix B, "An Overview of Problem Solving." A project in and of itself is a problem to be solved or a task to be accomplished.

As a student or team of students begins work on a project, participants are faced by the challenge of breaking the big problem (the overall project) into manageable subproblems or tasks. They are faced by the challenge of allocating and managing their resources (such as their personal time and access to IT) so that the subproblems and tasks are solved or accomplished in a timely fashion.

It takes quite a lot of training and experience for a student to learn to make a detailed outline of the steps needed to accomplish a project. Thus, students will need a lot of help as they begin to grapple with this task.

Milestones

A milestone is a clearly defined measure of accomplishment of the task or subtask. We will illustrate milestones using a simple IT-assisted PBL example. Suppose the whole class is engaged in a project to develop a newsletter in which each student will write a short article. Each student will use a digital camera to take a picture to be included with the article. The overall project might be envisioned as consisting of the following tasks:

1. Each student is to use a word processor to write a short article about his or her favorite animal, food, or toy.

   Milestone: First draft completed.

2. Each student is to learn how to use the digital camera and to move a picture from the camera into a word-processor file.

   Milestone: The student's word-processor file includes his or her picture to be used with the article.

3. Each student is to provide feedback to at least two other students on the articles these students have written.

   Milestone: Each student has received constructive feedback from at least two students and the teacher.

4. Each student is to edit his or her article based on feedback from multiple sources.

   Milestone: The article is edited based on feedback.

5. Tasks 3 and 4 are to be repeated as many times as necessary.

   Milestone: Each student has produced a well-written article.

6. Individual students polish their articles for publication.

   Milestone: The article with a picture is completed and ready to publish.

7. The teacher helps a team of students whose members are particularly adept at desktop publication to combine all the student articles and pictures into a class newsletter.

Milestone: Each student receives a copy of the newsletter.

This level of detail may be helpful as students first learn to plan and carry out IT-assisted PBL. Eventually, students will learn to chunk a number of steps into a single task. For example, perhaps tasks 1–6 would be represented by the following single task: Write an article that contains a picture you have taken using a digital camera.

Resources

In most projects, time is a limited and critical resource. In the newsletter project from the previous section, some of the other required resources include a digital camera, computers, Web access, a printer, and (perhaps) a copy machine. If there is only one digital camera, this may force the allocation of a long period of time for completing the picture-taking task.

A common pitfall for both teachers and students is to not allocate enough resources (especially time) to provide for unforeseen difficulties. What happens if a team member is ill? What happens if a particular task proves to be more difficult than anticipated? What happens if a necessary piece of equipment is out for repair? A robust plan includes a contingency-fund allocation of time and other resources. The teacher needs to be flexible, perhaps making major changes in an overall IT-assisted PBL lesson due to unforeseen difficulties.

Timeline

Because time is usually a critical and limited resource, it is important to develop a timeline that shows how the time resource will be allocated. When undertaking a multiday, time-limited project, one can analyze the various tasks, estimate how long each will take, and determine the order in which the tasks need to be done. Some aspects of this are easy to do, while others are quite difficult. For example, it is clear that one cannot do the final desktop publication and printing of a report before the report is written. But how long does it take to do the final desktop publication and printing of a two-page report? A student may face the problem that there is only one printer to serve 25 students; therefore, printing delays will be common.

It is often useful to develop a Task/Timeline Chart like the one in Figure 5.2, which is designed for a project to be carried out over a five-day period. The project consists of five tasks to be done sequentially. Thus, Task 1 is to be done on Day 1, Task 2 on Day 2, and so on. Note that the details on the actual tasks to be done or the milestones and the milestone dates have not been inserted.

FIGURE 5.2

A simple Task/Timeline Chart.

	Day 1	Day 2	Day 3	Day 4	Day 5
Task 1	XXXX				
Task 2		XXXX			
Task 3			XXXX		
Task 4				XXXX	
Task 5					XXXX

This type of Task/Timeline Chart works well as long as the project is linear. Figure 5.3 charts a linear four-task project designed to be carried out over seven days. Note that some of the tasks in this project require more than one day to complete. To save space, the columns for the Task Description and the Milestones have been omitted.

FIGURE 5.3

Another example of a Task/Timeline Chart for a linear project.

	Day 1	Day 2	Day 3	Day 4	Day 5	Day 6	Day 7
Task 1	XXXX	XXXX					
Task 2			XXXX				
Task 3				XXXX	XXXX	XXXX	
Task 4							XXXX

The example given in Figure 5.3 represents an increased challenge to both the teacher and the students. Some students work much faster than others. How does the teacher deal with the student who reports that "I am all done; now what should I do?" after a single day on Task 1 or Task 3? How does a student learn to allocate two days or three days of time to complete a lengthy task? Among other things, this requires learning to stop in the middle of a task and come back to it the next day.

Task/Timeline Charts become more complex when they are used to represent planning information for more complicated projects. Suppose that for the project represented in Figure 5.3, Task 2 could be done on any one of Days 1–6. Perhaps Task 2 is to use a digital camera to take several pictures to be inserted into a document. This creates a situation in which there could be a number of possible Task/Timeline Charts for the project. Figure 5.4 illustrates this situation.

FIGURE 5.4

Multiple Task/Timeline Charts for a project.

	Day 1	Day 2	Day 3	Day 4	Day 5	Day 6	Day 7
Task 1		XXXX	XXXX				
Task 2	XXXX						
Task 3				XXXX	XXXX	XXXX	
Task 4							XXXX

	Day 1	Day 2	Day 3	Day 4	Day 5	Day 6	Day 7
Task 1	XXXX	XXXX					
Task 2			XXXX				
Task 3				XXXX	XXXX	XXXX	
Task 4							XXXX

**FIGURE 5.4
(Continued)**

Multiple Task/Timeline Charts for
a project.

	Day 1	Day 2	Day 3	Day 4	Day 5	Day 6	Day 7
Task 1	XXXX	XXXX					
Task 2				XXXX			
Task 3			XXXX		XXXX	XXXX	
Task 4							XXXX

	Day 1	Day 2	Day 3	Day 4	Day 5	Day 6	Day 7
Task 1	XXXX	XXXX					
Task 2					XXXX		
Task 3			XXXX	XXXX		XXXX	
Task 4							XXXX

Things get even more complex when there are multiple tasks, some of which can be overlapped, and the time required to complete a task may be shorter than the time window in which it must be completed. One way to represent such a project is shown in Figure 5.5. To save space, columns for the Task Description and the Milestones have been omitted. In this case, Milestone Dates need to be at or after the block of time allocated to a task that has a milestone.

FIGURE 5.5

Task/Timeline Chart for
overlapping components of
a project.

	Length of task	Day 1	Day 2	Day 3	Day 4	Day 5	Day 6	Day 7
Task 1	2 days	XXX	XXX					
Task 2								
Task 2.1	1 day			XXX	XXX	XXX		
Task 2.2	1 day				XXX	XXX		
Task 3	1 day						XXX	
Task 4	1 day						XXX	XXX
Slippage	1 day							

There is a well-developed methodology—called PERT—for planning complex projects. PERT stands for Program Evaluation and Review Technique. An example is given in Figure 5.6. Computer software is available to help develop and analyze a PERT diagram.

FIGURE 5.6

A PERT diagram.

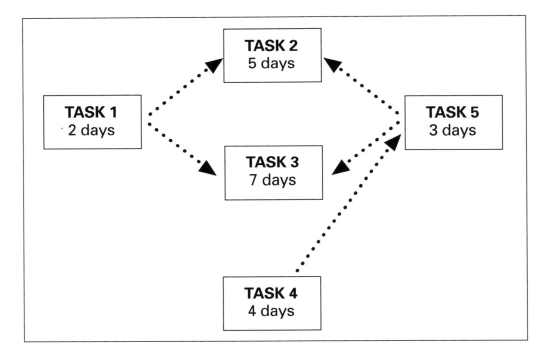

Planning the work of each individual and the collaborative work of a team adds still another dimension to the planning process. Consider a project in which teams of three students work together to produce hypermedia documents. A team consists of:

1. A team leader and hypermedia stack designer

2. A writer

3. A graphics and sound artist

Figure 5.7 shows a timeline for each team member. Part of the time the team members work together and part of the time they work individually. Notice that each team member has an individual task/timeline. If one team member fails to complete a critical task on time, the project will not be completed on time. Note that columns for Task Descriptions and for Milestones have been omitted to save space.

FIGURE 5.7

A Task/Timeline Chart for a team.

	A	B	C	D	E	F	G	H	I
1	Team Leader and Hypermedia Stack Designer								
2			Day 1	Day 2	Day 3	Day 4	Day 5	Day 6	Day 7
3	Task 1	Whole team planning	XXXX						
4	Task 2	Design the stack		XXXX	XXXX	XXXX			
5	Task 3	Whole team puts pieces together					XXXX		
6	Task 4	Whole team polishes final product						XXXX	XXXX

	A	B	C	D	E	F	G	H	I
1	Project Writer								
2			Day 1	Day 2	Day 3	Day 4	Day 5	Day 6	Day 7
3	Task 1	Whole team planning	XXXX						
4	Task 2	Research		XXXX					
5	Task 3	Write			XXXX	XXXX			
6	Task 4	Whole team puts pieces together					XXXX		
7	Task 5	Whole team polishes final product						XXXX	XXXX

	A	B	C	D	E	F	G	H	I
1	Project Graphics and Sound Artist								
2			Day 1	Day 2	Day 3	Day 4	Day 5	Day 6	Day 7
3	Task 1	Whole team planning	XXXX						
4	Task 2	Research		XXXX					
5	Task 3	Create art and sound			XXXX	XXXX			
6	Task 4	Whole team puts pieces together					XXXX		
7	Task 5	Whole team polishes final product						XXXX	XXXX

Final Remarks

One of the goals in IT-assisted PBL is for students to learn to undertake complex projects. This can be viewed as solving a complex problem or accomplishing a complex task. Thus, both general problem-solving strategies and domain-specific problem-solving strategies are applicable. You may find it helpful to browse through Appendix B, "An Overview of Problem Solving," for more information on this idea.

The project-planning ideas covered in this chapter constitute a general-purpose strategy that is useful over a wide range of projects. Every IT-assisted PBL lesson should be viewed as an opportunity for students to learn more about project planning and other aspects of carrying out a complex and challenging project.

Activities

1. Give several examples of when you have had to estimate how long it would take you to accomplish a major task. How accurate were your estimates? Suggest some ways for how one might get better at making estimates of the time required to carry out a complex task.

2. A number of the Task/Timeline Charts in this chapter allocate a specific amount of time for each task. For example, a student might have one day to do the Web research on a project or one day to write a first draft of a report on a project. Discuss the advantages and disadvantages of structuring the student's use of time this carefully. Include in your discussion the advantages accruing to students who have appropriate IT at home and good homework habits.

3. Try the following experiment with your students. Select a specific in-class or homework assignment. Have each of your students make a written estimate of how long he or she thinks it will take to do the activity. Collect the results and have the class work together to analyze them. Repeat this experiment several times with different in-class or homework assignments. A follow-up to this experiment is to have your students regularly make estimates (entered in their journals) of how long they feel a particular assignment will take to complete, and then how long it actually took. The goal is to improve your students' skill in estimating the time required to complete different tasks.

4. This chapter contains a number of Task/Timeline Charts that were created using a spreadsheet. Test your own knowledge and skills in use of a spreadsheet by creating a Task/Timeline Chart for a project that interests you.

CHAPTER 6

creating a PBL lesson plan

In creating, the only hard thing is to begin:
a grass blade is no easier
to make than an oak.

— *James Russell Lowell (1819–1891)*

This chapter begins with a discussion of some overall considerations in the development of a PBL lesson. It then presents a detailed, two-phase approach that can be used in creating a PBL lesson plan.

A Challenge to Teachers

Keep in mind that your overall goal as a teacher is to help accomplish the mission of your school and the educational system in which you work. IT-assisted PBL is merely a methodology, a means to an end. You have many other methodologies to help you.

There is substantial evidence that teachers tend to teach in the way they were taught. Since most teachers were taught in a didactic mode, it is only natural they would believe that the "stand and deliver" method is the best way to teach.

PBL is a more complex instructional tool than the lockstep, didactic instructional approach that has been so widely used during the past hundred years and more. PBL requires a considerable change in classroom management. The management of students nicely aligned in rows of seats and all reading or working on the same page of a book is different from the management of students working in groups, moving around the room to use various resources, and working independently on different projects.

Moreover, the use of IT in PBL adds still more challenge because the average teacher is unlikely to have a deep mastery of IT or of teaching in an IT environment. Thus, an initial decision to use PBL in an IT environment is a decision to stretch, to grow, to learn alongside one's students. Indeed, in stating goals for an IT-assisted PBL lesson, it is appropriate for the teacher to include some personal learning goals.

Finally, IT-assisted PBL requires a different approach to assessment than is used when all students are "covering" the same textbook materials. Chapter 7 discusses assessment.

As you gain knowledge and skill in developing and using IT-assisted PBL, you will find that it is an exhilarating and professionally satisfying approach to facilitating student learning. You will learn to be a "guide on the side" instead of being a "sage on the stage."

Some Universal Goals in an IT-Assisted PBL Lesson

The starting point for a PBL lesson is a topic or subject area, along with some specific educational goals and objectives. This is no different than developing a lesson plan to be carried out using some other method of facilitating learning.

An analysis of the topic, goals, objectives, and your own knowledge, skills, and teaching philosophy then leads to a decision about whether you will use IT-assisted PBL or some other teaching methodology. An experienced teacher has a wide repertoire of methods to facilitate learning. You should choose methods that best fit the needs of your students and the learning that you want to occur for you and your students.

In addition to having explicit goals and objectives for individual topics or subject areas, an IT-assisted PBL lesson contains several other very important explicit or implicit goals. For example, here are four student goals that should be part of every IT-assisted PBL lesson plan:

1. Students should get better at solving problems and carrying out complex tasks (see Appendix B, "An Overview of Problem Solving"). They should get better at working in a P/T Team environment.

2. Students should improve their higher-order and critical thinking skills and make use of their lower-order knowledge and skills.

3. Students should increase their knowledge and skill in undertaking a project and in using IT in a project environment (see Appendix A, "Goals for IT in Education").

4. Students should take increased responsibility for their own learning and work. They should make progress toward becoming independent, self-sufficient, lifelong learners and responsible workers.

All of these are "authentic" educational goals. That is, such goals are closely aligned with what it takes to solve real-world problems and perform well on a job.

Defining the Topic of a PBL Lesson

The first phase of developing a PBL lesson plan focuses on defining the topic of the lesson and analyzing the curriculum, instruction, and assessment. The following outline enumerates the areas you should consider.

1. Project content. Develop a working title or a mission statement for the project. Develop a brief summary of the content area. The summary includes answers to the following important questions:

    A. How does the project's content fit into the "big picture" of the overall subject being studied or the course of instruction? For example, if the project is being done in a history class, how does it fit in with the goals of the history unit or course? How does it fit in with the goal of helping students increase their expertise as historians?

B. How does the project contribute to being a component of a larger "mission"? Analyze it in these terms. (If you have trouble analyzing it in this way, the chances are that the project has weak authenticity.) Some examples of mission statements include the following: (i) to preserve our town's wetlands, (ii) to make our lake safe for swimming, (iii) to capture and preserve the history of our community, and (iv) to improve the quality of life of people in our community. Innumerable individual, team, and whole-class projects might be designed to contribute to accomplishing a mission.

2. Project goals. Briefly analyze the project in terms of how it relates to:

A. The general goals of education. Which specific goals of education are being focused on as students do the work of this project? (A brief summary of the goals of education is provided in Appendix A, "Goals for IT in Education.")

B. The general goals for IT in education. Which specific goals of IT in education are being focused on as students do the work of this project? (Goals for IT in education are also discussed in Appendix A.)

C. The specific goals within the content areas of the project.

3. Students' prerequisite knowledge and skills. Summarize your assumptions about the level of your students' knowledge and skills. Do all your students meet these prerequisites? How will you deal with situations in which individual students lack key prerequisite knowledge and skills?

4. Project teams. Formulate answers to questions such as these:

A. Will each student do an individual project or will there be multistudent teams? If there are teams, how will the teams be created? Will they include people from outside of the class, such as other students (perhaps even from other countries), parents, or mentors?

B. Assuming there are teams, what role will you play in specifying team leaders and each person's role on a team? For example, will you select teams so that they are balanced in strength and have diversity?

C. How will you deal with the situation of some students being unhappy with what team they are on or who is on their team?

5. Project timelines. Your planning in this area should include the following:

A. A timeline for the whole project, including an estimate of the number of minutes or class periods per day and the number of days, weeks, or months to be devoted to the project.

B. Checkpoint dates. What are the major milestones in accomplishing the project, and what are the dates by which these milestones are to be reached? What will students or teams be expected to present, show, or turn in as evidence of having reached the milestones?

6. Resources and materials.

A. What IT resources will the students and teams need? Are there constraints on the availability of these resources? For example, perhaps students will need to use a digital camera, but there is only one digital camera in the school. What happens if other classes also need to use this camera? What happens if it is broken sometime during the project?

B. What information resources do the students need to access? Will you have specific requirements on the number or nature of different information resources the students must use?

C. Will students be allowed or encouraged to use people as information resources? If so, how will this be facilitated, monitored, and referenced or attributed?

Work on items 1–6 can be carried out in a cyclic fashion. The process of working on a step will often suggest possible changes to the thinking you have done on other steps. As you near completion of your work on Items 1–6, finalize the project title and mission statement.

Implementing a PBL Lesson

This section contains a generic outline for implementing a PBL lesson. Of course, details will need to be adjusted to fit the specific topic, students, timeline, and other features of the project. The lesson-planning process consists of preparing yourself so you can follow the implementation steps.

This section is worded in a manner that assumes teams of students are each doing a project. With slight changes of wording, the same outline applies to individual students doing projects or to a team consisting of the entire class.

Getting Started

1. Define the topic. Share relevant information from the previous section, "Defining the Topic of a PBL Lesson." Facilitate a class discussion about the overall topic, timeline, choices available to students, and your expectations.

2. Establish timelines, milestones, and methods of assessment. What is the overall timeline for the project, what are the major milestones, and how will the project be assessed? Place special emphasis on individual and group responsibilities, and on individual and group assessment. When will you hold whole-class meetings in order to make modifications to timelines and to provide whole-class feedback or instruction? When will you provide feedback on what various groups or individuals are learning and the problems they are encountering?

3. Identify resources. What resources are available for use in the project? How will you or your students access scarce resources, such as a scanner, digital camera, or color printer?

4. Identify prerequisites and do advanced organizing. Schedule whole-class instruction and discussion focusing on:

   A. A review of how to define and carry out a complex, challenging project that requires use of multiple resources, higher-order thinking skills, and persistence over an extended period of time. What are the new challenges presented by this specific project?

   B. Any new non-IT content knowledge and skills students will need to carry out the project. The detailed lesson plan should include ways this learning will be facilitated.

   C. Any new IT knowledge and skills students will need to carry out the project. Again, the detailed lesson plan should include ways this learning will be facilitated.

   D. Learning about the goals of the project.

5. Form teams. Discuss when and where teams will meet. During or after the initial team meeting, provide time for teams to discuss Steps 1–4 and ask questions. Keep the focus on questions of interest to the whole class. When a question is quite specific to a particular team, suggest that the team will need to work on answering it and that you will be available later if the team needs help.

Initial Team Activity—Project Planning

6. Preliminary planning; pooling knowledge. Team members discuss the overall topic among themselves, sharing their knowledge about the topic and suggesting possible team projects.

7. Tentative specification of the team project. The team begins to define its specific project. This may require team members to do some research to increase their knowledge about potential components of the project. This will likely require interaction with the teacher.

8. Tentative specification of the project Task/Timeline Chart. The team is now relatively well organized. The overall project is broken into components, with individual responsibility and/or group responsibility assigned for each component.

9. Feedback from the teacher. The teacher provides feedback on the proposed team project, team organization, project Task/Timeline Chart, assignment of individual responsibilities, and assignment of group responsibilities. This is a major milestone.

10. Revisions to the plan. Based on feedback from the teacher and more careful consideration by the team members, the initial project Task/Timeline Chart is revised. It may be necessary to return to Step 9.

Project Implementation

11. Have students complete one task and milestone at a time. The project Task/Timeline Chart divides the project into a sequence of tasks, with each task having a timeline and milestone. Some tasks may involve a substantial amount of research by individual team members. Whole-team meetings in which the findings and progress are shared are an important part of a project.

12. Teams continually refine the project definition. As work on the project proceeds, the team should have time to reflect on the overall project and its goals. Minor revisions are a team matter. Major revisions may require returning to Step 9.

13. Team members take part in collaborative learning and cooperative problem solving. They share what they are learning and learn from each other. Team members work together to solve problems that arise.

14. Provide feedback. Students can do self-assessment and peer assessment. Individuals on the team monitor their own progress. Team members provide feedback to each other. Formative evaluation feedback comes from the teacher and from other sources. From time to time the teacher will likely provide feedback and instruction to the whole class based on observations about the work of an individual team.

15. Move toward completion. A project culminates in a product, presentation, or performance designed for a target audience. Team meeting time is needed to analyze how the various tasks are coming together and how the work of the individuals and team is progressing toward the final product, presentation, or performance.

16. Repeat steps 11–15 until all intermediate milestones have been reached.

Completion from the Student's Point of View

17. Final polishing. Students complete the project and polish the final product, presentation, or performance. They continue incrementally improving the final product, presentation, or performance as time and other resources permit.

18. Final assessment. The final product, presentation, or performance is turned in or done. Typically, the whole class is engaged in examining and using a product or viewing a presentation or performance. The whole class and the teacher provide constructive feedback. Feedback may also come from parents, other adults, and students in other classes.

    From a student's point of view, it is desirable that the completed project not be due until some time after the final presentation or performance. In that case, the student or team can incorporate feedback from students and others who view the final presentation or performance. One way to gain this feedback is for the student or team to develop a feedback form. This is given out to the audience viewing the presentation or performance. It is designed to provide feedback that the student or team will find useful in improving the product.

19. Individual and team closure. Individuals and teams analyze their final products, presentations, or performances and the feedback they have received. If the project has produced items to be added to student portfolios, time is provided for students to do portfolio development work and merge the project into their portfolios.

20. Whole-class closure. Facilitate a whole-class discussion on the project, including an analysis of ways to make the project better the next time it is used in a class.

21. Teacher closure. Record notes to yourself. Reflect on the project and make notes about what worked well and what needed improvement. Suggest changes you will try the next time you use this project with a class. Make some notes about what you learned working alongside your students.

Final Remarks

This chapter has provided thoroughly detailed lists of steps to follow in designing and implementing an IT-assisted PBL lesson. The chances are that you have already used some PBL in your teaching and that most of the steps seem like common sense to you.

Once you develop and implement a few IT-assisted PBL lessons, you will find that the overall process is relatively easy. Figure 6.1 provides a template designed to help you develop PBL lessons. The template is a general outline. You may find it necessary to adjust the template to your specific needs.

FIGURE 6.1

A PBL lesson plan template.

Learning Goal	Detailed Learning Objectives	Timeline and Milestones	Assessing the Learning Objectives	Resources Needed	Learning Prerequisites
1. Learn the subject matter content of the project	1a 1b 1c				
2. Learn IT as an integral part of the subject matter content	1a 1b 1c				
3. Learn some general aspects of IT not specific to your course	1a 1b 1c				
4. Learn to budget resources and to self-assess	1a 1b 1c				
5. Learn to work as a team member	1a 1b 1c				
6. Learn to be a project proposer, a problem solver, and a higher-order thinker.	1a 1b 1c				
7. Learn to transfer learning over time, distance, and environment.	1a 1b 1c				
8. Learn to learn and help others learn all of the above	1a 1b 1c				
9. Other (please specify)	1a 1b 1c				

Activities

1. Discuss similarities and differences between a "conventional" (non-PBL) lesson plan and the IT-assisted PBL lesson plan ideas presented in this chapter.

2. Develop an IT-assisted PBL lesson plan for a topic that interests you and that you feel will interest your students.

CHAPTER 7

assessment in IT-assisted PBL

The strongest memory is not as strong as the weakest ink.

— *Confucius (551 – 479 B.C.)*

As noted in Chapter 2, one of the defining characteristics of IT-assisted PBL is that both the content and the assessment are authentic. Authentic assessment is substantially different from traditional assessment that is based on objective and short-answer questions, and on essay questions.

This chapter focuses on authentic assessment of IT-assisted PBL. Successful implementation of authentic assessment requires education of the key stakeholders as well as development of authentic curriculum and instruction (National Foundation for the Improvement of Education, 1997). This means that students need to learn about assessment and their roles in the assessment process.

Portfolios are often one component of authentic assessment. Increasingly, portfolios make use of digital storage; such a portfolio may be called an electronic portfolio.

Authentic Content and Assessment

Some teachers are quite comfortable using both traditional assessment tools and authentic assessment tools. Others will find that authentic assessment has a challenging learning curve. This chapter is designed to help teachers negotiate that learning curve.

While general goals for education and IT in education are relatively widely understood and accepted (see Appendix A), the same cannot be said for assessment. Should we have nationwide testing? Should graduation from elementary school, middle school, or high school be based primarily on student performance on exams? Should the exams be objective and short answer, or should assessment be authentic and performance-based? Are the testing methods valid, reliable, and fair? Are they equally fair to males and females, different minority groups, children with differing handicapping conditions, and other major categories of test takers?

Assessment is a complex field, and almost everybody has an opinion about what should be done. In recent years, ideas such as authentic assessment, performance-based assessment, and portfolio assessment have received a lot of attention. At the same time, many school districts and states have placed renewed emphasis on the traditional paper-and-pencil tests, some of which are now administered by computer, perhaps in a computer-adapted testing mode (Applied Measurement in Education, 1992; Barrett, 1994; Brewer, 1996; Educational Leadership, 1992: Fogarty, 1996; Meng & Doran, 1993; Rothman, 1995; The Computing Teacher, 1994; Wiggins, 1993a, 1993b, 1996–97). Some states (such as Oregon, with its emphasis on a 10th-grade Certificate of Initial Mastery and its 12th-grade Certificate of Advanced Mastery) have combined traditional and authentic assessment at the statewide level and for college entrance.

The teacher doing assessment in an IT-assisted PBL lesson needs to think about the purpose of the assessment. This will help shape the evaluative information that will need to be gathered and the way this evaluative information will be used in the assessment.

There are many different stakeholders in an educational system. Examples include students, educators, parents, taxpayers, school boards, and the government. These various stakeholders have differing views on the goals or purposes of assessment. Three common purposes for assessment in education are:

1. To obtain information needed to make decisions. Different stakeholder groups often have different information needs and make different types of decisions based on the assessment information received. Assessment designed to fit the needs of students (arguably, the most important stakeholders) may be quite a bit different from assessment designed to meet the needs of teachers or government officials.

2. To motivate the people or organization being assessed. It is often said that student assessment drives the curriculum. Student success on state, national, and international tests serves as an affirmation to students, teachers, school administrators, and other stakeholders. This motivates teachers to "teach to the test" and motivates students to orient their academic work and studies specifically toward performing well on tests.

3. To emphasize accountability of students, teachers, school administrators, and the overall educational system. For example, a school district's educational system might be rated on the percentage of its students who graduate from high school or how well its students do on college entrance exams. Poor student performance may lead to major changes of administration and instructional strategies in the school district.

Sometimes the purpose of an assessment can be categorized on a scale like the one given in Figure 7.1. This scale runs from "Very Low Stakes" to "Very High Stakes." The "stakes" may be for a student, but they may also be for the teacher, school, or school district. Indeed, it has now become common to rank some schools or school districts as "failing" and to take actions based on this failure.

FIGURE 7.1

A "stakes" scale.

1 ········· 2 ········· 3 ········· 4 ········· 5

Very
Low
Stakes

Very
High
Stakes

The students' stakes are modest as a teacher wanders purposefully around the classroom, watching students work in groups on a project. The teacher makes mental and written notes (perhaps using a handheld personal digital assistant) about activities of individuals and the groups.

The students' stakes are likely to be somewhat higher on major projects that engage students over a period of weeks. A significant portion of a student's grade may depend on producing a newsletter that is carefully researched, designed, written, and desktop published.

Assessment can be for really high stakes. As an example, consider states that have implemented tests that students must pass in order to graduate from high school. As another example, a particular college may require that applicants score above a specified level on an entrance exam. Regardless of the student's previous record of achievements, failure to achieve above this specified level on the test results in the student not being admitted to the college. This is certainly an assessment with high stakes for the student.

Both the students and the teacher should have a clear understanding of the level of the stakes in a particular assessment. That is one important aspect of authentic assessment.

Assessing the Lesson Goals

Assessment in IT-assisted PBL needs to be closely aligned with the goals of the lesson. These goals may be much broader than the goals in a more traditional lesson plan.

Both a traditional lesson and an IT-assisted PBL lesson will have content or product goals. In the IT-assisted PBL lesson, the content or product goals are apt to be interdisciplinary. They will, of course, include IT goals as well as the goals of having students learn to work individually and/or on a team in designing and carrying out a project. Thus, the content or product goals may be more complex and varied than in a traditional lesson.

An IT-assisted PBL lesson typically has a number of process goals. Examples include cooperative learning, collaborative problem solving, self-feedback and peer feedback, and learning to function in a community of scholars. In IT-assisted PBL, all such goals are made explicitly clear to the students, as well as how the goals will be assessed.

Compared to a traditional lesson, an IT-assisted PBL lesson tends to have more goals and more varied goals. Thus, assessment tends to require more careful planning in advance of lesson implementation.

Feedback and Assigning Grades

Learning requires feedback. A learner has many different sources of feedback, including self, peers and other students, teachers, parents and other adults, teaching materials (for example, an answer key or answers given in computer-assisted learning), and so on.

In many cases this feedback is not connected to formal evaluation and grading of a student. This is important to keep in mind in an IT-assisted PBL lesson. Both feedback (to facilitate learning) and assessment (part of the teacher's job that provides important feedback to the teacher and others) are essential. Careful consideration needs to be given to each.

From a teacher's point of view, there are four common phases to the evaluation of an IT-assisted PBL activity.

1. Formative evaluation. Formative evaluation is designed to provide feedback while the student is still working on the project. This allows both the student and the teacher to make mid-project corrections. The teacher may use some of the formative evaluation information in a final assessment, but may choose not to do so.

2. Summative evaluation. Summative evaluation is carried out after the project is completed. A teacher might decide to base the project assessment purely on information gathered in the summative evaluation phase. However, a final assessment might also give considerable weight to the processes carried out in the project, such as accomplishing a project's milestones on time, the quality of intermediate products, and a student's effectiveness of participation in group processes.

3. Portfolio evaluation. A portfolio is a collection of work samples. Typically, a student and teacher work together to decide which work samples will go into the student's portfolio. During a school year, a large number of items may be collected for use in the school-year portfolio. Then some of them will be added to the student's long-term portfolio. The assessment of a student's overall work in high school might be based on an evaluation of a portfolio containing work done in high school.

4. Residual impact evaluation. With respect to the learning that occurs in a project, what does the student remember and what can the student do weeks, months, or years after the project has been completed? What can the student transfer to future studies, and to future work? Often a teacher does such evaluation in an informal manner. The teacher notes that as the year progresses, a student is getting better at cooperative learning, budgeting time, and taking pride in successful work. The teacher sees the student making use of ideas from one project in another project.

In an IT-assisted PBL lesson, both the students and teacher need to understand these four categories of evaluation and their possible roles in the assessment of the project and for other purposes, such as meeting graduation requirements, getting into college, or getting a job.

Overview of Evaluation

An IT-assisted PBL lesson is assessed by gathering a variety of evaluative data and information and then analyzing it to produce an assessment. The evaluative data and information will be both quantitative and qualitative. It will cover both the processes students carry out during the project and the final product, presentation, or performance.

Figure 7.2 provides a summary of the major areas in which one typically gathers evaluative data and information. Each of these three areas is briefly discussed in the following subsections.

FIGURE 7.2

Evaluation areas for IT-assisted PBL.

Evaluation Area	Comments
1. Subject area content goals of the project	The project content is often interdisciplinary. Usually, different students emphasize different aspects of the content area.
2. IT knowledge and skill content goals of the project	While a project may have IT as its primary goal, increased IT knowledge and skills are usually secondary goals. Different students frequently make considerably different uses of IT in a project.
3. Learning to do a project when working: A. individually B. in a group	Some projects are done individually, and some are done by teams. In a team project, there are typically both individual and team processes and components of the final product. Cooperative learning and collaborative problem solving are both very important in PBL.

Subject Matter Content Area

Suppose a history teacher is doing a unit on the Civil War in the United States. Students are to do a project that focuses on some important aspect of the Civil War and the historical time in which it occurred. The students are allowed to work individually or in small teams. The teacher observes the following situations:

- A team of four students chooses to create two newspapers that might have been published shortly after the battle at Gettysburg. One newspaper will be designed for publication in the North, while the other will be designed for publication in the South.

- One student decides to work alone to study the music of the Civil War, comparing and contrasting music of the North and South. This student intends to learn to perform music from the Civil War time period on the types of instruments available at that time.

- One student decides to work alone to study food and eating habits during the time of the Civil War. This student intends to learn to cook some traditional meals of that time.

- A pair of students decides to study clothing of the Civil War era and to create some "authentic" clothing.

It is easy to see that students will not all be learning the same thing. Moreover, the chances are that many of the students will gain knowledge that their teacher does not have.

However, all students will produce a product, presentation, or performance. The teacher has considerable knowledge about what constitutes a high-quality product, presentation, or performance and in most cases is qualified to evaluate the students' work. In special cases, the teacher may need to ask for help from other teachers or outside experts.

Moreover, as the history teacher continues to use PBL over a period of time, the teacher will acquire baseline data on the quality of the product, presentation, or performance that can be expected from students. The teacher will gain increased knowledge and skill about how to evaluate this type of student work. One of the values of PBL is that it helps to create a good learning environment for the teacher.

Presentations and performances are typically done for an audience, and the audience may be the whole class or an even larger group. A product (for example, a written document) also lends itself to sharing with a group. Thus, all students in a class can share in the products, presentations, and performances of their fellow class members. They can learn from the content of these activities. They can learn to evaluate these activities and provide constructive feedback. This is an important aspect of a PBL lesson.

In the Civil War example, the varied nature of the content areas the students will study precludes the use of traditional objective tests. Of course, the teacher may also assign some general background reading and other learning tasks to the entire class, and test students on these materials. This would lead to basing a student's grade on a combination of traditional and authentic assessment.

IT Knowledge and Skills

Some elementary schools have a computer specialist who gives students their first formal instruction in IT. However, in many elementary schools the regular classroom teacher is responsible for helping students develop their initial IT knowledge and skills. The teacher may have to give explicit instruction in the use of basic hardware and generic software tools.

This issue is complicated by the steadily increasing number of students who are learning about IT at home. Such students may enter school with a high comfort level in the use of a microcomputer, CD and DVD ROMs, and the Web.

Basic knowledge and skills about IT can be taught in a didactic manner. For example, if a teacher wants all students to know how to use a digital camera and a scanner to put graphics into a word-processed document, the teacher can do a whole-class demonstration and then provide individualized help as students try to apply what has been covered. Similarly, some uses of a microcomputer can be presented in a microcomputer lab, with whole group instruction followed by individual practice.

An alternative approach is to use peer instruction. One-on-one instruction might be provided by students in the class who have previously learned to use the equipment. Alternatively, the teacher may teach a small number of students how to use the camera and scanner, and then have these students serve as one-on-one teachers for the rest of the students in the class. Research strongly supports this approach. It is effective for the learners, and it is good for the students doing the teaching.

One of the goals in an IT-assisted PBL lesson is for students to increase their IT knowledge and skills. Thus, you (a teacher who is probably not an IT expert) must evaluate and assess this IT learning. A standard mistake that teachers tend to make in IT evaluation is to be overly impressed by the "Wow!" effect. This might best be described by a student making use of IT in a manner that seems rather spectacular and is beyond the teacher's current IT capabilities.

The reality of the situation may be that the IT use is something that is quite easy to learn and is being done at a very modest level. For example, a student might develop a slideshow that includes some video. Wow! Of course, the design of the overall slideshow and the individual slides may be terrible. The use of color, font, white space, and so on may violate the simplest principles of what is known about design for effective communication. The video might add little or nothing to the communication of the message. Still, the teacher might say "Wow!" and give the student high marks.

There are three general areas in which you might gather evaluative information in IT:

1. Students helping other students to learn IT. Here, you can observe students helping each other. You can see which students are in demand as helpers. You can see which students are frequently asking for help—perhaps repeatedly on the same topic.

2. Students learning IT on their own, from fellow students, at home, and at other locations. If a student's IT knowledge and skills are significantly better than might be expected from the level of instruction provided by the school, you can assume that the student is learning in other ways. Actual levels of knowledge and skills can be assessed through both pencil-and-paper tests and hands-on tests. In addition, you can observe a student using the IT facilities and gather data about the student's performance skills.

3. Students demonstrating IT knowledge and skills in their products, presentations, and performances. You can observe the results of student use of IT. In addition, you can look at electronic work samples (electronic copies of their work).

When you look at a printed desktop-published document, you cannot discern all of the underlying IT knowledge and skills the student has in the desktop-publishing area. You may not be able to tell if the student is using the word processor like an electronic typewriter or whether the student has gained the knowledge and skills of the desktop-publication field. For example, you cannot tell whether the student is using a first-line indent or a tab to indent at the beginning of a paragraph. You cannot tell if the student is following the desktop-publication rule of using only one blank space following the punctuation mark at the end of sentence. You cannot tell if a student has learned to use "styles" in doing word processing. For this kind of assessment, it is necessary for you to examine the student's work on a computer.

If you are just learning to use IT effectively, the chances are that you have not had much formal instruction in such areas as desktop publication, hypermedia design, design of effective interactive communication between a person and a computer, Web design and implementation, Web searches, and other areas. Thus, you probably are not well prepared to evaluate the details of this type of student work. Your learning will be greatly enhanced in this situation if you bring in an outside expert (perhaps a school district computer coordinator, an appropriate college or university faculty member, or a professional working in the field). Have the outside expert use a "think out loud" approach to evaluating the student work.

As you observe students doing IT work and look at their products, you will gradually see that some approaches are more effective and efficient than others. Gradually you will gain the knowledge and skills to help your students learn these aspects of IT, and you will learn how to evaluate the work your students are doing. Professional development and reading some of the literature can be very helpful. While there are many aspects of IT you can learn on the job by observing students at work and by working with students who have particular knowledge and skill in this area, there are other aspects that require formal instruction and study. IT is a large and challenging field!

Learning How to Do a Project

Figure 7.3 shows a Project Planning Table described in Chapter 5. Such a table provides a brief summary of some aspects of planning and carrying out a project.

FIGURE 7.3

A Project Planning Table.

	Description	Resources	Timeline	Milestones
Task 1				
Subtask 1.1				
Subtask 1.2				
Task 2				
Etc.				

As young students first begin to learn to carry out projects, you will do most of the project planning for them. It is not easy to visualize the sequence of steps needed to complete a long project. It is not easy to estimate how long it will take to carry out various tasks and subtasks. It is not easy to organize a team and allocate individual tasks to the various team members.

With instruction and practice, however, students will learn to take more and more responsibility for defining the topic, developing an outline of the tasks and subtasks, setting goals and milestones, deciding on needed resources, allocating the available resources, and completing a complex project in a timely and high-quality manner. With instruction and practice, students will learn to work individually and in a team to do complex projects.

Each project you assign should be designed to give your students the opportunity to maintain and improve their project skills. This means that in each project, you and others will need to gather evaluative information and provide feedback that will help students get better at doing projects.

For example, suppose you have decided that defining milestones will be emphasized in a particular project. Assume that this is a project in which there is considerable variety among the specific projects students are doing, and each student is doing an individual project. Each student will need to allocate his or her own time and other resources. Each student will need to set milestones and determine when the milestones are to be accomplished. An initial milestone is to describe the project to be done and to complete a Project Planning Table. You can then analyze a student's project description and Project Planning Table. You can provide written feedback, or you can discuss the project and Project Planning Table with the student. This feedback may lead to modifications in the project to be carried out and/or in the Project Planning Table.

The Project Planning Table is a useful evaluation instrument. You can expect a student to provide you with regular reports based on this table. These reports may include draft copies of various components of a project. They may include an analysis of barriers encountered and the ways the barriers are being overcome. The table may include a student's self-assessment of how the work on the project is going. If a team of students is working on a project, each student can be expected to provide feedback on how well he or she thinks fellow students are doing on project components that they are specifically responsible for.

Rubrics (Scoring Criteria)

One of the most important aspects of authentic assessment is that the students have a full understanding of the assessment criteria. Part of the learning that needs to go on in authentic assessment is for students to learn to understand the assessment criteria, learn to assess themselves, and learn to assess their fellow students.

A rubric is a scoring tool that can be used by students (for self-assessment and peer assessment), teachers, and others. It lists important criteria applicable to a particular type or piece of work. It also lists varying levels of possible achievement of the criteria. Figure 7.4 gives a very general-purpose, six-level scoring rubric. The next section in this chapter presents an adaptation of this general-purpose rubric to IT-assisted PBL.

FIGURE 7.4

A general-purpose, six-level rubric.

Level	Brief Description
1. Emergent	Student displays little, if any, of the expected rudimentary knowledge and skills.
2. Limited	Student displays rudimentary knowledge and skills but often requires substantial individual help and guidance.
3. Developing	Student displays a minimally adequate level of the expected knowledge and skills.
4. Capable	Student displays a functional, adequate level of the expected knowledge and skills.
5. Strong	Student displays a high level of the expected knowledge and skills.
6. Exceptional	Student displays an outstanding and creative/innovative level of the expected knowledge and skills.

It is common to use a Likert-type scale with an even number of levels for a rubric item. This forces the assessor to place the work into an "above the middle" or "below the middle" category.

The general-purpose rubric shown in Figure 7.4 needs more detail before it can be used in a particular assessment situation. For example, suppose you want to assess the writing component of an IT-assisted PBL lesson. Clearly, the meaning of the six points will be different for third-grade students than it will be for 12th-grade students. The levels have to be defined relative to what can reasonably be expected of students at a particular grade level.

In writing and in all the traditional subject matter areas, there is considerable information about what can be expected of students at various educational levels. In IT, however, this knowledge is just beginning to be developed. The National Educational Technology Standards discussed in Appendix A are reflective of these emerging guidelines. The performance indicators for the various grade levels are designed to show a much higher expectation for older students.

Rubrics have been developed for many different curriculum areas, and lists of these have been published (Brewer, 1996). Each wide-scale implementation of such rubrics has been accompanied by extensive research on their effectiveness as well as the nature and extent of teacher education needed for their effective use. Some of the conclusions supported by this research include the following:

- It is not easy to develop good rubrics. Wiggins (1996–97) discusses rubrics his research organization has developed. He emphasizes that the development of rubrics is a process that leads to a product; both the process (of developing rubrics) and the product (the resulting rubrics) should be assessed.

- Since curriculum, instruction, and assessment need to be aligned, scoring rubrics by themselves do not lead to an improvement in education. A substantial amount of professional development and significant changes in both curriculum and instruction are essential components of moving toward effective authentic assessment and improvements in education.

- Teachers need to learn to modify the scoring rubrics published in books and articles to better fit their own teaching situations and styles. They also need to learn to develop rubrics.

- The introduction of authentic assessment into a classroom, school, or school district may encounter considerable resistance from teachers, parents, students, and other key stakeholders. It represents a substantial change from "traditional" assessment, and many people oppose such change. As with any school reform project, all the key stakeholders need to be involved. There must be considerable emphasis on helping the stakeholders learn about the advantages of authentic assessment, as well as difficulties and drawbacks.

- Wide-scale use of authentic assessment requires a major investment in the assessment process. The assessors need to have a high level of competence and training. Achieving reasonably reliable results requires that several people assess a student product and that mechanisms exist for resolving discrepancies. Anyone who has watched the scoring of athletic performances in diving, gymnastics, or ice skating is familiar with this process. Each performance is scored by several judges, and the highest and lowest score is often thrown out. A head judge may call the judges together to discuss and resolve discrepancies.

A Sample IT Rubric

The next six subsections describe the six levels in a general purpose rubric for assessing student use of IT tools. The information on these six levels is quoted from a page (no longer available) of the Oregon Educational Technology Consortium Web site.

Level 1—Emergent Technology User

- Selected technology tools to assist in creating the desired product that were inappropriate for the task or student is not able to operate tool.

- Technology was used but not to benefit the creation of a quality product.

- Technology tools were tried by the student, but the required product could not be produced.

- Was unable to resolve most technological obstacles relating to the project.

- Ethical and professional behavior was not shown or was inappropriately shown through lack of citations, copyright adherence, and ethics.

Level 2—Limited Technology User

- Selected less effective tools from what was available to create the desired product.

- Technology was used to address the tasks but few of the capabilities of the technologies were used to create the product.

- Technology tools were used and set up appropriately, but only with major outside assistance.

- Was able to solve only elementary technological obstacles.

- Ethical and professional behavior was occasionally shown through appropriate citations, copyright adherence, and ethics.

Level 3—Developing Technology User

- Selected appropriate tools from what was available to create the desired product, but only with outside assistance.

- Technologies were used but assistance was needed for the basic capabilities of the technology to create the product.

- Technology tools were set up and used appropriately but required some outside assistance.

- Was able to solve most basic obstacles associated with the project.

- Ethical and professional behavior was generally shown through appropriate citations, copyright adherence, and ethics.

Level 4—Capable Technology User

- Selected adequate tools from what was available and appropriate for creating the desired product.

- Technology was used in an appropriate way and the basic capabilities of the technology were applied to create the product.

- Technology tools were set up correctly and used appropriately with minor assistance.

- Was able to solve some of the technology-related problems associated with the project.

- Ethical and professional behavior was shown through appropriate citations, copyright adherence, and ethics.

Level 5—Strong Technology User

- Selected quality tools from what was available to create a quality product.

- Technology was used in appropriate ways and many of the features were applied to create a quality product.

- Technology tools were set up correctly and used appropriately without assistance following established guidelines.

- Solved most technology-related problems associated with the project.

- Ethical and professional behavior was shown through appropriate citations in proper form, copyright adherence, and ethics.

Level 6—Exceptional Technology User

- Selected the most appropriate tools from what was available to create high-quality products.

- Technology was used in an innovative way to create a higher quality product than the assignment anticipated.

- Technology tools were not only set up correctly and used appropriately, but suggestions were also provided for improvement in the procedures.

- Solved all technology-related problems associated with the project.

- Ethical and professional behavior was shown through appropriate citations in proper form, copyright adherence, and ethics.

Notice that the last bulleted item in each list focuses of ethical and professional behavior. Most organizations that develop standards or goals for IT in education include this topic.

A Specific Desktop-Publication Example

This section contains a partial example of a scoring rubric that might be used in a unit of instruction in which students learn to design and desktop publish a newsletter. The main emphasis in the instructional unit is on students learning to use IT tools. However, there is also some emphasis on students learning to communicate effectively while using these tools.

The unit of instruction in this example is different from a writing unit in which the main emphasis is on effective written communication, with only minor emphasis on desktop publication of the resulting written document. Remember, assessment must be aligned with curriculum and instruction. Scoring rubrics that fit a unit emphasizing IT will necessarily be different from scoring rubrics that fit a unit emphasizing written communication.

In this particular unit, the students study a number of principles of design for an effective newsletter. The assumption is that they are already skilled in using a word processor, scanning and editing graphics, and printing documents.

The rubric shown in Figure 7.5 contains only some of the items that would be used for this newsletter project. No items having to do with the quality of the written content have been included. This particular example uses a six-level scale for each rubric item. Four-level scales are also commonly used. The intent is that the different levels form an equal interval scale.

It is evident that it takes considerable learning on the part of the students and teacher to use these rubric items effectively. The assessment, curriculum, and instruction are interwoven. The curriculum and instruction will include the examination of a number of different desktop-published newsletters. Students will practice assessing these newsletters, their own newsletters, and the newsletters of their fellow students.

Desktop Design and Publication

The student work displays:

1. No understanding and use of this principle.

2. A limited understanding and use of this principle.

3. A developing understanding and use of this principle.

4. A capable understanding and use of this principle.

5. A strong and creative understanding and use of this principle.

6. An exceptional and highly creative understanding and use of this principle.

FIGURE 7.5

Part of a rubric for a student newsletter project.

Principle	Level (Circle one)	Comments and Suggestions
Banner: communicates well, attracts and holds the reader's attention.	1 2 3 4 5 6	
Text: readable; limited number of typefaces; right amount of text.	1 2 3 4 5 6	
Text color and background color work together to enhance communication.	1 2 3 4 5 6	
Grid and alignment: clear and consistent pattern of use.	1 2 3 4 5 6	
White space: not too little or too much; used well, not trapped.	1 2 3 4 5 6	
Unity: text, graphics, and design work together.	1 2 3 4 5 6	
Visual scan: directs reader to important elements.	1 2 3 4 5 6	
Other principles as necessary.	1 2 3 4 5 6	

Electronic Portfolios

Portfolios and portfolio assessment have long been an important part of assessment in the graphic arts. Similarly, music students can record their performances, and dance and theater students can videotape their performances.

In recent years, the idea of using portfolios and portfolio assessment has spread to other disciplines. A portfolio might contain writing samples that illustrate changes in writing skill over a period of time. It might contain samples of science lab reports or written tests from any discipline. A student's hypermedia project can become a component of a portfolio.

Students can now carry out projects and develop products that can be adequately represented and used only on a computer. Interactive multimedia stacks and Web pages provide excellent examples of this new form of product. Student work done using a computerized music synthesizer, science simulations, and sophisticated mathematical software all support the need for electronic portfolios. Thus, portfolio items are increasingly created or transferred into digital format so that they can be stored in a computer-readable medium. Such a portfolio is called an electronic portfolio. Electronic portfolios have considerable advantages over other forms of portfolios in terms of offering ease of editing, making copies, and providing portability. However, viewing an electronic portfolio requires appropriate hardware, software, knowledge, and skills. Moreover, after a period of time, hardware and software change so that an electronic portfolio may no longer be readily usable.

Final Remarks

There are many challenges to a teacher first learning to do authentic assessment of IT-assisted PBL. For both the teacher and the students, this will be a learning process. It is a process in which the teacher and students can work together and learn from each other.

Activities

1. What are your personal feelings about authentic or performance-based assessment versus traditional assessment? From your personal experiences and point of view, present arguments for and against each approach and then summarize your current position.

2. Select an IT-assisted PBL lesson topic. Develop assessment rubrics that would be suitable for this lesson. Your rubrics should cover non-IT content, IT-content, and learning to work individually and on a team doing a project.

3. Consider the following assertion: A good rubric is one that students can both understand and use effectively for accurate peer and self-assessment. Discuss this assertion and your beliefs about it.

CHAPTER 8

the future of IT-assisted PBL

*When you're finished changing,
you're finished.*

— Benjamin Franklin (1706 – 1790)

The future of IT-assisted PBL is inextricably intertwined with:

1. The continuing rapid increase in the capabilities and availability of IT.

2. The steadily increasing importance of the P/T Team.

3. Professional development for educators.

4. Widespread public acceptance of the need to substantially improve our educational system.

This chapter explores some possibilities for the future of IT-assisted PBL in education.

A Brief History of IT in Education

In the United States, the first instructional uses of computers in precollege education occurred in the late 1950s. At that time, some students and their teachers began to learn to write computer programs that could be run on the computers available at nearby colleges and businesses. A modest number of secondary students learned to use the FORTRAN program language and punch cards.

During the 1960s, timeshared computing was developed, as well as the student-oriented BASIC programming language. Many precollege students had the opportunity to learn to write BASIC programs to solve simple problems, especially math and science problems.

Microcomputers began to come into schools in the late 1970s. In 1983 it was estimated that in K–12 education there was approximately one microcomputer for every 125 students. Now, nearly 20 years later, it is estimated that schools have approximately one microcomputer for every five students. Essentially all schools, and the majority of classrooms, have Internet connectivity. In addition, perhaps two-thirds of all students live in households where a microcomputer is available, and it is now common for such students to have Internet access from home.

In 1983, one could buy a complete microcomputer system for about $1,000. This system included an 8-bit, 1-megahertz machine with 64 K of primary memory, a 5.25-inch floppy disk drive, and a monochrome monitor. In 2002, one could buy a much better microcomputer system for well under $1,000. This system would include a 32-bit, 800-megahertz machine with 256 megabytes of primary memory, a 100 or 200 megabyte removable media Zip drive, a 24x CD-ROM drive, a 40-gigabyte hard drive, a 56 K modem, a 15-inch color monitor, and a color printer. The gain in cost/effectiveness over this 19-year span is overwhelming, not even taking into consideration the declining value of the dollar due to inflation.

It is now feasible to expect that all students will learn to use computers in school and that the use of computers will be integrated into a number of curriculum areas. The National Educational Technology Standards (see Appendix A) developed by the International Society for Technology in Education (1998) can be achieved with the quantity and quality of IT hardware, software, and connectivity available in many of today's schools.

Moreover, the past 10-15 years of technological change and availability of IT in schools is apt to continue for the next 10-15 years. (This is discussed in more detail in the next section.) Thus, the problems caused by inadequate hardware, software, and connectivity will continue to decline. It would be nice if we could comfortably predict similar success for IT in the overall curriculum, instruction, and assessment, and that the needed staff development will occur. That, however, remains problematic.

Computing Power and Connectivity in the Future

For more than three decades, the world has witnessed an exponential rate of growth in the amount of computing power that has been made available. There are two major components to this growth rate. First, there has been, on average, a 15 percent yearly increase (adjusted for inflation) in sales of microelectronics. Second, the cost of a given amount of computer power has been dropping 50 percent every 18 months. This decreasing cost is known as Moore's Law, named after Gordon Moore, one of the founders of Intel.

Many people predict that both of these trends will continue for the next 10-15 years or so. If these predictions turn out to be correct, worldwide production of computer power 15 years from now will be more than 8,000 times the current level. Such numbers tend to be overwhelming. The simple meaning is that we had better educate our students for adult life in a society that will provide routine access to a huge amount of computer power!

In recent years we have been experiencing even faster growth in the bandwidth and amount of worldwide connectivity. We all know that the Internet is continuing to grow in capacity and in the number of users it is serving. The telecommunications capacity of the world is growing relatively rapidly, and fiber optics is one of the reasons. There is ongoing research to improve the capacity of glass fiber. In 2002 a company successfully demonstrated the ability to transmit about 2.5 terabits per second over a single fiber that was 2,500 miles long.

A speed of 2.5 trillion bits per second is 1,000 times the speed of the fastest commercial fiber optic systems in use in 1996. Even without data compression, such a speed would allow the transmission of two hours of video across the country in less than two seconds.

One of the characteristics of our current science and technology is how rapidly the research results are implemented in actual practice. Internet2 is designed to make effective use of high-bandwidth data transmission, with speeds more than 1,000 times that of Internet I. This initiative is already reaching into K–12 and precollege education (**www.internet2.edu**).

Revisiting the Problem/Task Team

The Problem or Task Team (P/T Team) discussed in Chapter 1 is a central idea in IT-assisted PBL. Variations of this idea have been with us for quite a while. For example, Perkins (1992) discusses Person Plus (a person using tools) as one of the most important ideas in education. Figure 8.1 shows a schematic of the P/T Team structure.

FIGURE 8.1

The P/T Team structure.

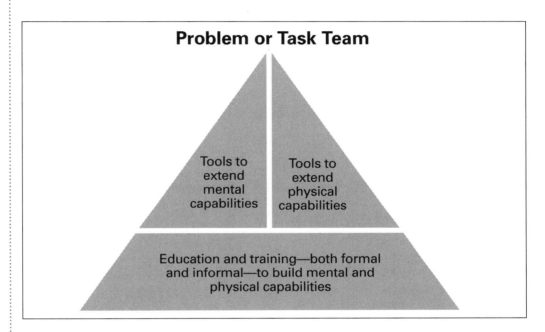

Our educational system is struggling with what to do about the ideas embodied in the P/T Team. For example, consider the impact of a simple four-function calculator. Although the National Council of Teachers of Mathematics recommended the use of calculators in math education in 1980 (and again in the standards published in 1989), it is only in the past few years that the use of calculators has been allowed on national exams, such as college entrance exams. We are probably many years away from the time when the use of a microcomputer will be routine in testing situations.

However, a modest number of K–12 schools and colleges are now requiring that all their students have a portable microcomputer. They are experimenting with allowing or requiring the use of microcomputers in all classes and on tests. The groundwork is being laid for the time when such computer accessibility and use will be common. In the world of business and industry in the United States, the number of available microcomputers available for use in "white collar" jobs now exceeds the number of workers holding such jobs.

The Information Explosion

Most of us are already overwhelmed by the amount of data and information that is available. Estimates of the global growth rate of accumulated data and information suggest that we may experience a doubling every five years, or perhaps even more rapidly. Think about this from the point of view of a child just starting school. A doubling every five years means an increase by a factor of eight before the student finishes college. Clearly, a "rote memory" approach to education is futile.

The World Wide Web can be thought of as a combination of a communication and storage system. It is both a tool for accessing the rapidly growing Global Digital Library and a storage mechanism for this library.

The information explosion and the rapid increase in the capabilities of the Web will continue far into the future. IT provides some assistance in dealing with the information explosion. However, this assistance requires changes in our educational system—in our curriculum, instruction, and assessment. For starters, think about the knowledge and skills of a well-trained research librarian. This person knows how to find information and how to tell good information from bad information. Now think about helping all students begin to gain such knowledge and skills, starting at the earliest grade levels. This is beginning to emerge as one of the goals of education. In the future, it will be an even more clear-cut and important goal.

Adoption of IT Innovations

While we can predict with some confidence that more and better IT will be available on a worldwide basis, this does not mean that schools will embrace this innovation. Everett Rogers (1995) has spent his professional career studying the adoption of innovations. His book (now in its fourth edition) is a treasure trove of stories about innovations that have been adopted and innovations that have not been adopted.

Rogers begins his book with a story about the innovation of boiling drinking water in a Peruvian village. All of the sources of water in this village were polluted. Typhoid and other water-borne diseases were a serious and continuing health problem. The health services in Peru undertook a two-year campaign to convince the 200 families in the village of the benefits of boiling their drinking water to help prevent disease.

The innovation was backed by solid scientific research. When the intervention began within the village, it was supported by 15 families who were already boiling their drinking water. The intervention itself included a medical doctor who visited the village to give talks on the importance of boiling one's drinking water and a local public health worker who devoted a great deal of time to the project.

Nevertheless, the innovation was not widely adopted. The two-year intervention resulted in only 11 additional families adopting the innovation of boiling their drinking water.

This Peruvian village has been extensively studied. Why was the innovation of boiling drinking water not widely adopted? The next section helps answer this question and considers some educational implications for IT.

A Culture Is Hard to Change

The Peruvian village had a deep-seated culture. The details of the culture are not particularly important. What we know is that a culture—be it in a village, corporation, or school—is hard to change. Many educators have been slow to embrace IT, perhaps because it represents a significant change in some culture.

Think about a school as a culture. It has students, administrators, teachers, and support staff. It has classrooms, subject matter areas, and time schedules. It has lectures, reading, homework and other assignments, and tests. It has parents who went to similar schools. All the major stakeholders—students, teachers, school administrators, parents, school board members, and government officials—are familiar with this culture, and most are supportive of it.

Suppose that just one of the stakeholders attempts to make a significant change in the culture. When this is a top-down (government or school board) or bottom-up (student or teacher) approach, it is not likely to succeed. The existing culture is a careful and long-standing balance among the various stakeholders. Any unilateral attempt to change the balance (change the culture) meets with resistance from the rest of the stakeholders.

IT-assisted PBL requires that a teacher change from being a "sage on the stage" to being a "guide on the side." However, the "sage on the stage" concept and a didactic model of instruction are strongly ingrained in the educational culture. This suggests that the following approaches may help a teacher to successfully make a change toward increased use of IT-assisted PBL:

- Work with young students who have not yet learned that a teacher is a sage on the stage. Young students are still learning about the roles of teachers, and they can just as well be learning that a teacher has a dual role of being both a sage on the stage and a guide on the side.

- With older students, use the innovation at the beginning of a course (or at the beginning of a new unit). Indicate to the students that the course or unit content and the methodology are thoroughly intertwined—new course, new methodology.

- Educate parents and other stakeholders.

- Take advantage of any movements toward authentic assessment and portfolio assessment occurring in your school, school district, or state. Remember, authentic assessment requires authentic curriculum, and IT-assisted PBL is one form of authentic curriculum.

- Take advantage of any movement toward block scheduling in your school. Longer time periods for classes fit in well with PBL.

- Take advantage of the movement toward having individual classrooms with pods of four or five computers. This makes it much easier for students to do IT-assisted PBL.

- Take advantage of the information explosion. Every IT-assisted PBL lesson should be viewed as an opportunity for students to improve their research skills. There is widespread agreement among educational stakeholders that these are valuable skills.

- Take advantage of the "trialability" (the opportunity to conduct small trials) of IT.

One of the key ideas in Everett Rogers' book is the "trialability" of an innovation. Can a potential adopter try the innovation without making a full and major investment or commitment in the innovation?

Fifteen years ago, it was not easy for a teacher who wanted to make innovative instructional use of IT. Access to the needed hardware, software, and connectivity was difficult to obtain. Student knowledge about IT was low. The threshold for getting started (for conducting a trial) was high.

Gradually, however, the threshold has been lowered. The early adopters have led their schools to having a substantial amount of hardware, software, and connectivity. Students have learned about IT at school and at home, so they have an increasing base of knowledge and skills. Large numbers of teachers own a computer, and educators as a whole have a significant and growing personal knowledge about using IT.

It appears that conditions are now ripe for relatively wide-scale adoption of IT-assisted PBL. Many teachers already know about PBL (but not about IT-assisted PBL) and have experience in using it in their teaching. It is a relatively small step to try IT-assisted PBL. This step can be made by using whatever current IT knowledge and skills the teacher and his or her students have, and whatever hardware, software, and connectivity is available to them.

A Summary of Some Important Ideas

Here is a brief summary of some of the key ideas covered in this book.

1. IT-assisted PBL can be used at all grade levels and in all subject areas. It is a powerful and versatile aid to curriculum, instruction, and assessment. The process of doing a project includes:

   A. Project posing—defining the project. What are the specific goals and objectives? Are the goals balanced among learning important subject matter, improving higher-order thinking skills, and learning to function well in a Person Plus environment? How can one measure progress toward and appropriate accomplishment of the goals and objectives?

   B. Resource allocation. Identify the available resources (including time).

   C. Planning. Analyze the various components of the project, clearly specifying what is to be accomplished in each component. Develop a plan for how resources are going to be allocated to accomplish the plan. Develop a plan for the order in which different components must be accomplished. Which components can be done in parallel, and which must be completed before others can be started?

   D. Implement the plan. This often begins with doing substantial research using multiple sources of information. Implementation may require learning to do new things, such as learning how to conduct an interview or how to use specific pieces of hardware and software. Implementation often requires repeatedly returning to Step A and refining the project based on what is being learned as work on the project progresses.

   E. Continual improvement. A project culminates in a product, presentation, or performance designed for a target audience. A product, presentation, or performance can be incrementally improved. There is an excellent parallel with process writing, mncremental improvement of consumer products in business, and rehearsal or practice in sports and the performing arts.

2. Creative problem solving can be taught. IT-assisted PBL provides an excellent environment in which students can improve their creative problem-solving skills. Important ideas in problem solving include the following:

A. Build on your own previous work and the previous work of others.

B. View each problem or project as a learning opportunity. As you solve a problem or accomplish a task, work to learn things that will help you in the future. Do metacognition; do reflective thinking; do conscious, considered analysis of the components and the overall process for each major problem you solve.

C. Through study, practice, metacognition, and reflective thinking, students can increase their expertise in solving hard problems and accomplishing hard tasks.

3. Students engaged in IT-assisted PBL can use available hardware and software effectively. There should be an emphasis on students developing knowledge and skills in using generic software tools, such as an integrated package that includes a word processor, graphics (draw and paint) application, database, spreadsheet, graphing feature, and telecommunications components (Web and e-mail). Students should also learn to use presentation and hypermedia software. In IT-assisted PBL lessons there should be an emphasis on:

A. Learning to learn. This includes learning from one's fellow students and helping one's fellow students learn. It includes "just in time" learning.

B. Working on a team to accomplish a challenging task. This includes learning to take responsibility for one's own work and for the work of the entire team.

4. Authentic assessment is an essential component of IT-assisted PBL. With appropriate instruction, practice, and encouragement, students can become skilled at self-assessment and peer assessment. Teachers and students can work together as they learn about and engage in authentic assessment.

5. There is a growing research base to support the use of PBL and IT-assisted PBL in education. Strong support for PBL is emerging from research in brain theory, learning theory, the study of multiple intelligences, and the study of constructivism and situated learning theory.

6. Many schools and individual teachers currently structure their time within a school day in a manner that is not supportive of IT-assisted PBL. Generally speaking, a project requires sustained blocks of time. There appears to be some movement on the part of schools and individual teachers toward restructuring their time schedules to provide these longer blocks of time.

7. The P/T Team is an important idea in education and is a powerful change agent. IT-assisted PBL is a good way to help students learn to function well in a P/T Team environment.

8. IT-assisted PBL is an excellent approach for teachers taking increased responsibility for their own professional growth and development.

Final Remarks

Many educational leaders feel that professional development is the key to improving our educational system. Our educational system needs to be changed to significantly increase the opportunity for classroom teachers to participate in professional evelopment. Professional development needs to be an ongoing activity; it should be part of the day-to-day, week-to-week life of a teacher. Every teacher needs to be a lifelong learner.

IT-assisted PBL can be one piece of this needed professional development. Remember, one of the goals of an IT-assisted PBL lesson is to facilitate teacher learning on the job!

Activities

1. Analyze your current level of IT-assisted PBL use. What are the major barriers to increasing this level of use? What can you do to overcome these barriers?

2. Suppose that your school had a microcomputer for every student and teacher, that these microcomputers were 100 times as fast as the current ones, and that they were all connected to the Web using a bandwidth that supports real-time, full-screen video. (All of this is likely to be true in many schools 15 years from now.) How would this affect your job as a teacher and the overall education of students in your school?

goals for IT in education

IT-assisted PBL is an educational vehicle. It is an aid to accomplishing the mission and goals of education and of IT in education. The first part of this appendix contains a brief summary of the overall goals of education. The remainder focuses specifically on goals of IT in education. An IT-assisted PBL lesson should be supportive of the overall goals of education and should include one or more goals aligned with the goals of IT in education.

Overall Goals of Education

David Perkins (1992) provides an excellent overview of education and a description of the wide variety of attempts to improve our educational system. He analyzes these attempted improvements in terms of how well they have contributed to accomplishing the following three major goals of education:

- The acquisition and retention of knowledge and skills.

- An understanding of one's acquired knowledge and skills.

- An active use of one's acquired knowledge and skills (the ability to apply one's learning to new settings; the ability to analyze and solve novel problems).

These three general goals—acquisition, understanding, and the use of knowledge and skills—help guide formal educational systems throughout the world. They provide a solid starting point for the analysis of any existing or proposed educational system.

The next three subsections expand on Perkins' three goals and cover ideas that should be incorporated into every IT-assisted PBL lesson.

Acquisition and Retention

The totality of information stored in the world's libraries is increasing exponentially. Estimates of the doubling time vary, with some people suggesting a doubling of information every five years. The United States Library of Congress adds more than 5 million documents every year to its collection.

A person's knowledge is a combination of information and understanding of the information that the person has processed and stored in his or her mind. Knowledge is constructed or assimilated—that is, it is based on previous knowledge and understanding.

We all agree that data and information can be stored in a computer. Steady progress in artificial intelligence, computer hardware, and computer software raises the question of the nature and extent of a computer system having knowledge. Some people argue that knowledge is something that a person can have but that a machine cannot have. Others argue that both people and machines can have knowledge, and that eventually we will produce computer systems that "know" more than people.

The distinction between information and knowledge is important. Memorizing more and more information does not, in and of itself, provide a person with more knowledge. The information has to be integrated into existing knowledge and processed or assimilated into usable forms. That is the essence of constructivism, which is strongly supported by research into brain theory.

The amount of knowledge one can acquire and retain includes a very tiny fraction of the totality of the information humans have collected and stored—and this fraction is rapidly decreasing. An alternative to trying to acquire more information is to develop the skills of a research librarian. Learn to make effective use of the emerging Global Digital Library, which can be accessed through computer networks.

Research—seeking out, analyzing, and finding new information—is a component of any good PBL project. Students learn to use multiple sources of information. They learn to deal with ambiguity, conflicting information, and inadequate information. They learn to design and conduct research projects that lead to increases in the total amount of information that humans have discovered and developed.

Understanding and Analysis

One of the criticisms of our current educational system is that many students can regurgitate memorized information but they have little or no understanding of the meaning of the information. Rote memory is no substitute for understanding.

Similarly, the ability to retrieve information from a library is no substitute for understanding what one retrieves. Our educational system must substantially increase its emphasis on understanding and higher-order thinking skills.

A good PBL lesson requires substantial use of higher-order thinking skills. Thinking, analysis, creativity, problem solving—these are required in every project. A project provides an authentic context for understanding and using the information one is acquiring and turning into knowledge.

Active Use of Knowledge and Skills

A PBL lesson includes a focus on creating a product, presentation, or performance. Students use their knowledge and skills and then demonstrate what they have done. The audience may be rather narrow, for example, just the teacher and students in a class. However, the audience may be much broader and include other students, parents, the community, or people throughout the world.

IT in schools empowers students. Given appropriate opportunities and facilitation, students can accomplish tasks and solve problems that were beyond the capabilities of adults before computers and other IT became available. Students can address real-world problems and produce useful results.

Standards

The three relatively short goals for education certainly represent an oversimplification of education. Perhaps the other end of the scale is represented by the education standards that have been developed by many different organizations, working in many different subject areas. Substantial information about state and national education standards is available at **http://otec.uoregon.edu/national_standards.htm**.

An Overview of IT in Education

The diagram in Figure A.1 presents an overview of the uses of IT in K–12 education.

FIGURE A.1

IT uses in K–12 education.

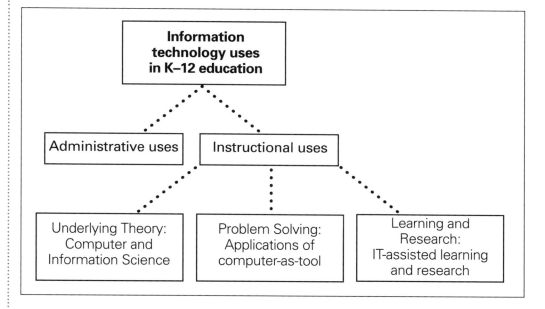

This diagram divides education into two major components—administration and instruction. Each uses IT extensively. There is a strong parallel between administrative uses of computers in schools and in business. In administrative uses of IT, educators have learned a lot from business people.

However, this section focuses only on instructional uses of IT. In instructional uses, educators have often taken the lead in helping business people learn about IT.

It is important to understand the major differences among the three main instructional-use categories of IT. Many misunderstandings about IT in instruction can be resolved through an analysis of these three categories, which are described in the next three subsections as if they are separate and distinct. In many applications, these categories overlap. Students seldom engage in using IT that falls purely into only one of the three categories.

Computer and Information Science

Over the past 50 years, computer and information science has emerged as a major discipline of study. Many community colleges, technical institutes, colleges, and universities offer degree programs in this discipline. There is a relatively high demand for workers who have good knowledge and skills in computer and information science. Detailed information about the field of computer and information science is available at the Association for Computing Machinery Web site **www.acm.org**.

A number of high schools offer an Advance Placement (AP) course in computer science. The course prepares students to take an AP test; students may receive college credit if they score well on this test. The course offers a balance between the theory and practice in the field, and it includes considerable emphasis on computer programming. Sometimes this course is offered as a two-year sequence designed to cover roughly the equivalent of a one-year university course. Only a very small percentage of students take an AP computer science course in high school. The great majority of K–12 students receive little or no formal instruction in this academic discipline.

The Computer as a Tool

The computer is a useful and versatile mind tool. It can be used to help solve problems and accomplish tasks that are at the center of many different academic disciplines. Computer tools for use in education can be divided into three categories:

1. Generic tools. Software programs such as word processors, spreadsheets, database managers, graphics packages, e-mail, and Web browsers cut across many disciplines. A student who learns to use these tools can apply them in almost every area of intellectual work.

2. Subject-specific tools. There are tools designed for a particular academic discipline, for example, hardware and software that aids in musical composition and performance. Software for doing mechanical drawing (computer-assisted design) is another widely used subject-specific tool. Many different disciplines have developed hardware and software specifically to meet the needs of professionals within those disciplines.

3. Learner-centered tools. There are tools that require some programming skills but that also focus on learning to learn and on learning subjects besides programming. Most hypermedia and Web authoring systems serve as examples. Many of the generic tools include a built-in "macro" feature that adds learner-centered options. Both database managers and spreadsheets usually have such capabilities.

Progress in developing more and better application packages, as well as better human-machine interfaces, is causing the use of the computer as a tool to grow rapidly. Also, computer scientists working in the field of artificial intelligence (AI) are producing application packages that can solve a variety of difficult problems that require a substantial amount of human knowledge and skill. Such application packages will eventually change the content of a variety of school subjects.

The key issue is what students should learn to do mentally versus what they should learn to do assisted by simple aids such as books, pencils, and paper versus what they should learn to do assisted by more sophisticated aids such as calculators, computers, and other IT. This is a difficult question, particularly given the constantly changing state of technology. The slow acceptance of the handheld calculator into the curriculum suggests that more sophisticated aids to problem solving will encounter substantial resistance. The gap between what tools are available and what tools are used in education is likely to increase.

The computer can also be a tool that increases teacher productivity. Computerized gradebooks, data banks of exam questions, computerized assistance in preparing individual education plans (IEPs) for students with disabilities, and word-processed lesson plans and class handouts are all good examples. These increase teacher productivity by improving overall efficiency of effort and saving valuable time. This is particularly true as networks allow teachers to easily find and share successful materials.

Many teachers now use a desktop presentation system as an aid to interacting with a group or whole class of students. This is a projector system attached to a computer. It can be used to display prepared materials or graphs and other materials generated during the interaction between students and the teacher. For example, in a math class, the computer and projection system can be used to create and project a graph of data or a function being explored by the students and the teacher.

IT-Assisted Learning and Research

This section combines ideas about three very important uses of IT in education. Computer-assisted learning (CAL) is the interaction between a student and a computer system designed to help the student learn. Computer-assisted research is the use of IT as an aid to doing library and empirical research. Distance learning is the use of telecommunications designed to facilitate student learning.

Some people attempt to make a clear distinction between CAL and distance learning. They emphasize the role that human teachers often play as teachers in distance learning courses. Others note that CAL can be delivered over the Internet and that the "teacher" presenting distance learning may be a videotape or a computer-generated character.

Over the past 40 years, CAL has been given many different names, such as "computer-based instruction" and "computer-assisted instruction." In recent years, the concept has come to include distance learning, e-mail-based instruction, and Web-based instruction. The acronym CAL is intended to emphasize *learning* rather than just *instruction*. CAL includes drill and practice, tutorials, simulations, and a variety of virtual reality environments designed to help students learn.

The computer can be used for instructional delivery at every age, in every subject area, and with all types of students. Evidence is mounting that CAL is especially useful in special education and basic skills instruction (Kulik, 1994). In addition, CAL and distance education can provide students with access to courses not available in a teacher-delivered mode in their schools.

There are two major categories of computer-assisted research at the K–12 level. First, there is the use of computers to search the Web and read CD-ROM and DVD-ROM materials. Students of all ages can gain some of the knowledge and skills of the research librarian. Second, there is the use of computerized instrumentation to gather data. Many middle school and secondary school students are learning to use microcomputer-based laboratory tools.

Distance learning is rapidly growing in use and importance. There are now two commonly used approaches to this. In synchronous distance learning, students and instructors can be connected in a two-way audio and a one-way or two-way video network that allows real-time interaction. This is essentially the same as videoconferencing. Increasingly, distance learning is asynchronous (not real-time) and is delivered over the Web. This adds convenience for the student. In the typical Web-based course, students interact with each other and the instructors (students often do group projects), even though they may be located at different places around the world.

Educational Technology Standards

Many schools, school districts, and states have set scope and sequence goals for IT in education.

At a national level, the International Society for Technology in Education has developed National Educational Technology Standards (NETS) for K–12 students (International Society for Technology in Education, 1998). All the information in the remainder of this section is quoted from the ISTE NETS document.

ISTE National Educational Technology Standards for Students (NETS·S)

This subsection lists the six ISTE standards for education technology and gives some general goals for each standard.

Standard 1. Basic operations and concepts:

- Students demonstrate a sound understanding of the nature and operation of technology systems.
- Students are proficient in the use of technology.

Standard 2. Social, ethical, and human issues:

- Students understand the ethical, cultural, and societal issues related to technology.
- Students practice responsible use of technology systems, information, and software.
- Students develop positive attitudes toward technology uses that support lifelong learning, collaboration, personal pursuits, and productivity.

Standard 3. Technology productivity tools:

- Students use technology tools to enhance learning, increase productivity, and promote creativity.
- Students use productivity tools to collaborate in constructing technology-enhanced models, preparing publications, and producing other creative works.

Standard 4. Technology communication tools:

- Students use telecommunications to collaborate, publish, and interact with peers, experts, and other audiences.
- Students use a variety of media and formats to communicate information and ideas effectively to multiple audiences.

Standard 5. Technology research tools:

- Students use technology to locate, evaluate, and collect information from a variety of sources.
- Students use technology tools to process data and report results.
- Students evaluate and select new information resources and technological innovations based on the appropriateness to the specific tasks.

Standard 6. Technology problem-solving and decision-making tools:

- Students use technology resources for solving problems and making informed decisions.
- Students employ technology in the development of sophisticated strategies for solving problems in the real world.

The next four subsections contain performance indicators for different grade levels of students. Each performance indicator is tied to one or more of the six standards listed above.

Grades PK–2

Prior to completion of Grade 2, students will:

1. Use input devices (e.g., mouse, keyboard, remote control) and output devices (e.g., monitor, printer) to successfully operate computers, VCRs, audio tapes, and other technologies. (1)

2. Use a variety of media and technology resources for directed and independent learning activities. (1, 3)

3. Communicate about technology using developmentally appropriate and accurate language. (1)

4. Use developmentally appropriate multimedia resources (e.g., interactive books, educational software, elementary multimedia encyclopedias) to support learning. (1)

5. Work cooperatively and collaboratively with peers, family members, and others when using technology in the classroom. (2)

6. Demonstrate positive social and ethical behaviors when using technology. (2)

7. Practice responsible use of technology systems and software. (2)

8. Create developmentally appropriate multimedia products with support from teachers, family members, or student partners. (3)

9. Use technology resources (e.g., puzzles, logical thinking programs, writing tools, digital cameras, drawing tools) for problem solving, communication, and illustration of thoughts, ideas, and stories. (3, 4, 5, 6)

10. Gather information and communicate with others using telecommunications, with support from teachers, family members, or student partners. (4)

Grades 3–5

Prior to completion of Grade 5, students will:

1. Use keyboards and other common input and output devices (including adaptive devices when necessary) efficiently and effectively. (1)

2. Discuss common uses of technology in daily life and the advantages and disadvantages those uses provide. (1, 2)

3. Discuss basic issues related to responsible use of technology and information, and describe personal consequences of inappropriate use. (2)

4. Use general-purpose productivity tools and peripherals to support personal productivity, remediate skill deficits, and facilitate learning throughout the curriculum. (3)

5. Use technology tools (e.g., multimedia authoring, presentation, Web tools, digital cameras, scanners) for individual and collaborative writing, communication, and publishing activities to create knowledge products for audiences inside and outside the classroom. (3, 4)

6. Use telecommunications efficiently and effectively to access remote information and communicate with others in support of direct and independent learning, and pursue personal interests. (4)

7. Use telecommunications and online resources (e.g., e-mail, online discussions, Web environments) to participate in collaborative problem-solving activities to develop solutions or products for audiences inside and outside the classroom. (4, 5)

8. Use technology resources (e.g., calculators, probes, videos, educational software) for problem-solving, self-directed learning, and extended learning activities. (5, 6)

9. Determine when technology is useful and select the appropriate tool(s) and technology resources to address a variety of tasks and problems. (5, 6)

10. Evaluate the accuracy, relevance, appropriateness, comprehensiveness, and bias of electronic information sources. (6)

Grades 6–8

Prior to completion of Grade 8, students will:

1. Apply strategies for identifying and solving routine hardware and software problems that occur during everyday use. (1)

2. Demonstrate knowledge of current changes in information technologies and the effect those changes have on the workplace and society. (2)

3. Exhibit legal and ethical behaviors when using information and technology, and discuss consequences of misuse. (2)

4. Use content-specific tools, software and simulations (e.g., environmental probes, graphing calculators, exploratory environments, Web tools) to support learning and research. (3, 5)

5. Apply productivity/multimedia tools and peripherals to support personal productivity, group collaboration, and learning throughout the curriculum. (3, 6)

6. Design, develop, publish, and present products (e.g., Web pages, videotapes) using technology resources that demonstrate and communicate curriculum concepts to audiences inside and outside the classroom. (4, 5, 6)

7. Collaborate with peers, experts, and others using telecommunications and collaborative tools to investigate curriculum-related problems, issues, and information, and to develop solutions or products for audiences inside and outside the classroom. (4, 5)

8. Select and use appropriate tools and technology resources to accomplish a variety of tasks and solve problems. (5, 6)

9. Demonstrate an understanding of concepts underlying hardware, software, and connectivity, and of practical applications to learning and problem solving. (1, 6)

10. Research and evaluate the accuracy, relevance, appropriateness, comprehensiveness, and bias of electronic information sources concerning real-world problems. (2, 5, 6)

Grades 9–12

Prior to completion of Grade 12, students will:

1. Identify capabilities and limitations of contemporary and emerging technology resources and assess the potential of these systems and services to address personal, lifelong learning, and workplace needs. (2)

2. Make informed choices among technology systems, resources, and services. (1, 2)

3. Analyze advantages and disadvantages of widespread use and reliance on technology in the workplace and in society as a whole. (2)

4. Demonstrate and advocate for legal and ethical behaviors among peers, family, and community regarding the use of technology and information. (2)

5. Use technology tools and resources for managing and communicating personal/professional information (e.g., finances, schedules, addresses, purchases, correspondence). (3, 4)

6. Evaluate technology-based options, including distance and distributed education, for lifelong learning. (5)

7. Routinely and efficiently use online information resources to meet needs for collaboration, research, publications, communications, and productivity. (4, 5, 6)

8. Select and apply technology tools for research, information analysis, problem solving, and decision making in content learning. (4, 5, 6)

9. Investigate and apply expert systems, intelligent agents, and simulations in real-world situations. (3, 5, 6)

10. Collaborate with peers, experts, and others to contribute to a content-related knowledge base by using technology to compile, synthesize, produce, and disseminate information, models, and other creative works. (4, 5, 6)

Second-Order Effects of IT in Education

The ISTE NETS project described previously specifies goals for IT in education. Future work on this project will lead to the development of guidelines for integration of IT throughout the curriculum, for staff development and support systems, and for student assessment. This section presents one possible approach to specifying the desired levels of student use of IT.

Initially, most new technology is used to do essentially the same thing as the old technology, but it accomplishes a task or solves a problem in a better way. This impact can be thought of as an amplification of what is already being done. The initial new technology may not be a significant improvement on the old. For example, the early horseless carriages (cars) were in many ways not as good as a traditional horse and carriage because the horse could follow a road or path with little help from the driver, while the horseless carriage needed the driver's full attention. Nevertheless, the horseless carriage had the potential to be significantly better than horses in accomplishing the task of moving people and materials.

For any invention that becomes widely used, we often see three stages of adoption and use. First, the invention is improved to the point where it is clear that it has significant advantages. That is, it becomes an effective amplification over the previous technology and offers better methods of solving a particular problem or accomplishing a particular task. For example, horseless carriages improved in their reliability and speed.

Second, the infrastructure needed for widespread use of the invention begins to develop. In the current example, cars became more useful and more widely used as an infrastructure of paved roads, filling stations, and repair people was developed.

Finally, second-order effects begin to emerge. Use and impact of the invention moves beyond amplification. The outward spread of cities and shopping malls were second-order effects of cars, as was air pollution from exhaust fumes. Other second-order effects included the development of superhighways, a trucking industry, and a worldwide petroleum industry. There was a fundamental change in the transportation industry.

There are many first- and second-order effects in IT. Here are some examples that are particularly relevant to education. A major goal in PBL is to move students into routine use of the second-order levels of IT.

- The use of a computer to do word processing is a first-order effect, an amplification of the electric typewriter. The use of the full capabilities of a word processor produces second-order effects. For example, students can use an outliner, spelling checker, graphics, and the various aids to desktop publication as they produce documents that effectively communicate their messages.

- The use of a computer to insert simple graphics into a word-processed document is a first-order effect. The use of a computer to create and/or edit animation, photographs, sound, and video are all second-order effects. Interactive hypermedia is another second-order effect. As IT has continued to improve, it has become possible for elementary school students to develop hypermedia projects. The challenge to elementary school teachers is obvious. IT in K–12 education has had the second-order effect of overwhelming our inservice educational system. Curriculum, instruction, and assessment are not changing nearly as rapidly as the technology that is being provided to students.

- The use of a computer to do business payroll computations is a first-order effect. The spreadsheet is a second-order effect. The spreadsheet facilitates the development of computer models of a business, and these models can be used to do forecasting and to examine "what if?" types of questions. Initially, the spreadsheet was viewed as an accounting tool, so its use was gradually integrated into high school business courses. However, spreadsheets have proven to be a very useful modeling and computational tool in many different academic disciplines and grade levels, even down into the elementary school level. Moreover, modern spreadsheet software includes an extensive set of graphing capabilities, which is a powerful aid to analyzing, representing, and communicating information.

- The use of an electronic calculator or a computer to do simple mathematical and scientific calculations is a first-order effect. By the late 1970s, calculators were reliable and inexpensive enough so that students at some schools were routinely using them. We are now seeing the second-order effects of electronic calculators: major changes in the curriculum and students being allowed to use calculators on college entrance exams. For example, graphing calculators have been thoroughly integrated into much of the mathematics curriculum at the upper levels of secondary school and in higher education. Eventually, we will see computers thoroughly integrated into the curriculum and being used in national assessments.

- The use of a computer to directly gather data from a scientific experiment is a first-order effect. Use of a computer to control the experiment is a second-order effect. Laboratory instrumentation has become increasingly sophisticated. Instruments now exist that can quickly and automatically solve problems that used to take researchers many hours of time. Computers also now allow real-time control of sophisticated research experiments.

Another second-order effect is the use of the microcomputer-based laboratory (MBL) as a teaching and learning tool. In an MBL, students use IT-based laboratory instrumentation, such as a computer connected to various measuring devices. Students design and carry out experiments, the computer gathers the data, and then students direct the computer in an analysis of the data. Many students at the middle school level and higher are learning science through this hands-on approach, which includes using sophisticated but inexpensive instrumentation.

- A computer can solve many of the types of problems that occur in mathematics, science, and engineering. Computers and sophisticated calculators quickly achieved the first-order effect of replacing paper and pencil, slide rules, and simple calculators to do these computations. But, computers make possible the three-dimensional mathematical modeling of molecules, airplanes, nuclear explosions, and other complex problems studied by scientists and engineers. These second-order effects are changing what students need to learn to be effective scientists and engineers.

- The use of a computer to send and receive electronic mail is a first-order effect. The World Wide Web is a second-order effect. Teams of people working together through desktop conferencing and groupware are another second-order effect. Our schools are just beginning to develop the curriculum, instruction, and assessment needed for an environment in which students have routine access to the Web. Few students are learning to learn and solve problems in a groupware environment. Groupware is an important component of Person Plus.

- Another second-order effect of computer networks is that worldwide networking facilitates international competition for an increasing number of jobs. If a job can be accomplished by telecommuting, then perhaps the worker can live 10,000 miles from company headquarters. The second-order effect in education is a gradual emergence of worldwide standards. Students throughout the world need an education that adequately prepares them for jobs that exist throughout the world.

- An electronic encyclopedia on a CD-ROM is a first-order effect. The emerging Web-based Global Digital Library is a second-order effect. In the past, elementary school teachers faced the challenge of helping students gain a functional level of knowledge and skill in using a card catalog by the time they left elementary school. Now, elementary school teachers face the more difficult challenge of helping students use the Global Digital Library effectively.

- The use of a computer to automate flash cards is a first-order effect. This is a widely used form of computer-assisted learning. Immersion of a learner in a highly realistic and interactive computer simulation or virtual reality designed to facilitate learning is a second-order effect. Similarly, the use of e-mail to facilitate receiving and sending lessons in a distance education course is a first-order effect. Interactive Web-based distance education courses are a second-order effect. Students need to learn to learn in these computer-assisted learning and distance learning environments.

- The use of computers to digitize, store, and play back sound is a first-order effect. The use of computers to create and edit sounds is a second-order effect. The music industry has been greatly changed by computer technology. The facilities needed to compose, edit, and play electronic music are now available to many schoolchildren, even at the elementary school level. This presents a significant challenge to our music education system.

The distinction between first-order and second-order levels of IT use is not a finely divided line. The second-order levels of use tend to represent major transformations in the nature of how information is processed, how problems are solved, and how people communicate (Pea, 1985). PBL lessons can and should be designed to facilitate both first-order and second-order levels of IT use.

The question arises as to whether students need to move through the first-order levels before they engage in the second-order levels of IT. Many adults take this approach and assume that this is also necessary for children. However, many teachers have found that their students are quite capable of moving directly into the second-order levels of IT.

Final Remarks

The field of IT in education is just beginning to emerge from its infancy. There is growing agreement on IT standards for students at the precollege level. There is growing awareness that such standards can be achieved only by integrating IT into the content of all academic disciplines.

Currently, there are approximately five students for every microcomputer in our K–12 schools. More than half of this equipment is in classrooms, and much of it has Internet accessibility. Eventually there will be enough IT facilities so that students can routinely use this hardware and software at their own convenience.

While access to facilities continues to be a major barrier to IT in education, teacher training and the integration of IT into the everyday curriculum, instruction, and assessment are larger barriers. IT-assisted PBL can help overcome these barriers.

an overview of problem solving

This appendix gives a brief overview of the "subject" of problem solving and of roles of IT in problem solving. It is targeted specifically toward preservice and inservice teachers. The ideas from this appendix can be woven into instruction in almost any curriculum area.

This appendix focuses both on solving problems and on accomplishing tasks. We will use the term problem solving to include all of the following:

- Posing and answering questions
- Posing and solving problems
- Posing and accomplishing tasks
- Posing and making wise decisions
- Using higher-order, critical, and wise thinking to do all of the above

Our educational system attempts to differentiate between lower-order cognitive (thinking) skills and higher-order cognitive (thinking) skills. In recent years there has been increased emphasis on higher-order skills. In very brief summary, we want students to learn some facts, but we also want them to learn to think and solve problems using the facts.

Often the "thinking" that we want students to do is to recognize, pose, and solve complex, challenging problems. Thus, one of the goals of education is to help students to get better at posing, representing, and solving problem. A few schools actually offer specific courses on problem solving. For the most part, however, students learn about problem solving through instruction in courses that have a strong focus on a specific content area. All teachers teaches problem solving within the specific subject matter areas of their curriculum.

Many people have observed that the "every teacher teaches problem solving" approach is haphazard, and that the result is that students do not get a coherent introduction to problem solving. When a student reaches a specified grade level, can the teacher be assured that the student has learned certain fundamental ideas about posing, representing, and solving problems? Can the teacher assume that a student knows the meaning of the terms problem, problem posing, and problem solving? Can the teacher be assured that the students know a variety of general purpose strategies for attacking problems? In our school system at the current time, the answer to these questions is "no."

Thus, teachers are left with the task of helping their students master both the fundamentals of problems solving and then the new problem-solving topics that each teacher wants to cover. This appendix covers the basics (fundamentals) of problem solving. It is designed as a general aid to teachers who need to cover the fundamentals with their students.

Of course, the fundamentals need to be interpreted and presented at a grade-appropriate level. This appendix does not try to do that. It is left to individual teachers to understand the fundamental ideas and then present them in a manner that is appropriate to their students.

This appendix places particular emphasis on several important problem-solving ideas:

1. Posing, representing, and solving problems are intrinsic to every academic discipline or domain. Indeed, each discipline is defined by the specific nature of the types of problems it addresses and the methodologies it uses in trying to solve problems.

2. There are some tools (for example, reading and writing) that are useful in addressing the problems in all disciplines. IT provides us with some new and powerful tools that are useful aids to problem solving in every discipline.

3. Much of the knowledge, techniques, and strategies for posing, representing, and solving problems in a specific domain requires a lot of knowledge of that domain and may be quite specific to that domain. However, there are also a number of aspects of posing, representing, and solving problems that cut across many or all domains, and so there can be considerable transfer of learning among domains. Our educational system should help all students gain a reasonable level of knowledge and skill in these broadly applicable approaches to problem solving.

Problem and Task Team

Donald Norman is a cognitive scientist who has written extensively in the area of human-machine interfaces. Norman (1993) begins with a discussion of how tools (physical and mental artifacts) make us smart. David Perkins (1992) uses the term Person Plus to refer to a person making use of physical and mental tools. In many situations, a person with appropriate training, experience, and tools can far outperform a person who lacks these aids.

In this appendix we use the term Problem or Task Team (P/T Team) to refer to a person or a group of people and their physical and mental tools. Figure B.1 illustrates the P/T Team. These concepts are explained in subsequent paragraphs.

FIGURE B.1

The P/T Team—People aided by physical and mental tools.

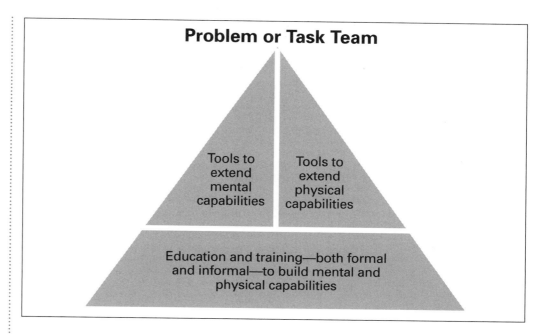

Figure B.1 shows a person or a group of people at the center of a triangle with three major categories of aids to solving problems and accomplishing tasks:

1. Mental aids. Even before the invention of reading, writing, and arithmetic (about 5,000 years ago) people used notches on bones, drawings on cave walls, and other aids for counting and keeping track of important events. Reading, writing, and arithmetic are mental aids. These have led to the development of books, math tables, libraries, calculators, computers, and many other mental aids. Mental aids supplement and extend the capabilities of a person's mind.

2. Physical aids. The steam engine provided the power that led to the beginning of the Industrial Revolution. Well before that time, however, humans had developed the flint knife, stone ax, spear, bow and arrow, plow, hoe, telescope, and many other aids to extend the physical capabilities of the human body. Now we have cars, airplanes, and scanning electron microscopes. We have a telecommunications system that includes fiber optics, communications satellites, and cellular telephones.

3. Educational aids. Education is the glue that holds it all together. Our formal and informal educational systems helps help people learn to use the mental and physical tools as well as their own minds and bodies.

IT is a combination of both mental and physical aids. One way to think about this is the use of computers to automate factory machinery. Such machinery stores or contains a certain type of knowledge, and the machinery can use that knowledge to carry out certain manufacturing tasks. An artificially intelligent, computerized robot provides another example of a combination of mental and physical tools.

The mental and physical aids components of a P/T Team are dynamic, with significant changes occurring over relatively short periods of time. The pace of change of IT seems breathtaking to most people.

On the other hand, our formal educational system has a relatively slow pace of change. This has led to the interesting situation in which many preschool children grow up with routine access to mental and physical aids, learning their use through our informal educational system and then encountering formal education that is woefully inadequate in dealing with such aids. For example, many elementary school students have more IT knowledge and skill than do their teachers.

In our current society, people who are skilled at functioning well in a P/T Team environment have a distinct advantage over those who lack the knowledge and skills developed in this environment. Such analysis leads to the recommendation that the P/T Team and problem solving should be a central themes in education.

Domain Specificity

Each academic discipline focuses on a category of problems that help to define the discipline and methodologies for solving these problems. Chemistry, history, and mathematics are different disciplines because they address quite different types of problems and have developed quite different methodologies for addressing problems.

Moreover, each academic discipline has a huge amount of accumulated knowledge. A mathematician can spend a lifetime studying a specific subdomain such as algebra, geometry, or statistics, and not fully master just one specific subdomain. A musician cannot hope to gain a high level of expertise in each musical instrument and type of music. Similarly, an artist cannot hope to gain a high level of expertise in each art medium.

Research into problem solving has indicated that one needs considerable domain-specific knowledge and skills to pose, represent, and solve problems within that domain. People use the term *domain specificity* when discussing this idea. Thus, it is not surprising that that formal education is usually broken up into specific courses that focus on specific components of specific domains. This approach allows courses to be designed and taught by people who are relatively competent in the subject matter domain of the course.

Domain specificity is a major challenge to our educational system. For the most part, real-world problems cut across different domains. Thus, we teach students in a domain-specific manner and environment and expect that they will transfer their knowledge and skills to the interdisciplinary problems they encounter outside of school. This is a huge leap of faith, and what actually happens is that relatively few students make such transfers of learning.

Fortunately, the situation is not quite as bleak as it sounds. While many aspects of problem solving are domain specific, there are also many ideas about problem solving that cut across all domains. Thus, with appropriate education and experience, a person can gain some general expertise in problem solving that is useful in addressing any new problem that he or she might encounter.

Moreover, there has been a gradual increase in the understanding of how to teach for transfer. That is, progress in the domain of transfer of learning has begun to provide teachers with specific information about how to teach for transfer.

What Is a Formal Problem?

There is a substantial amount of research literature as well as many practitioner books on problem solving (Frensch & Funke, 1995; Moursund, 2002; Polya, 1957).

Problem solving consists of moving from a given initial situation to a desired goal situation. That is, problem solving is the process of designing and carrying out a set of steps to reach a goal. Usually the term *problem* is used to refer to a situation where it is not immediately obvious how to reach the goal. The same situation can be a problem for one person and not be a problem (instead, just a simple activity or routine exercise) for another person. Figure B.2 graphically demonstrates this concept.

FIGURE B.2

Problem-solving—How to achieve the final goal.

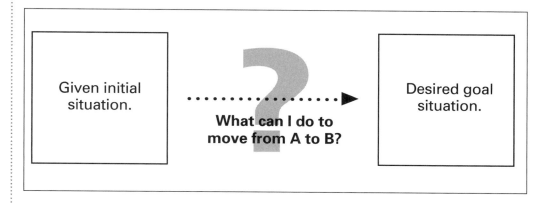

Here is a formal definition of the term *problem*. You (personally) have a problem if the following four conditions are satisfied:

1. You have a clearly defined, given initial situation.

2. You have a clearly defined goal (a desired end situation). (Some writers talk about having multiple goals in a problem. However, such a multiple-goal situation can be broken down into a number of single-goal problems.)

3. You have a clearly defined set of resources that may be applicable in helping you move from the given initial situation to the desired goal situation. There may be specified limitations on resources, such as rules, regulations, and guidelines for what you are allowed to do in attempting to solve a particular problem.

4. You have some ownership—you are committed to using some of your own resources, such as your knowledge, skills, and energies, to achieve the desired final goal.

These four components of a well-defined problem are summarized by the four words: *givens, goal, resources,* and *ownership*. If one or more of these components are missing, we call this a *problem situation*. An important aspect of problem solving is realizing when one is dealing with a problem situation and working to transform that into a well-defined problem.

People often get confused by the resources part (part 3) of the definition. Resources do not tell you how to solve a problem. Resources merely tell you what you are allowed to do and/or use in solving the problem. For example, you want to create a nationwide ad campaign to increase the sales by at least 20 percent of a set of products your company produces. The campaign is to be completed in three months, and it is not to exceed $40,000 in cost. Three months is a time resource and $40,000 is a money resource. You can use the resources in solving the problem, but the resources do not tell you how to solve the problem. Indeed, the problem might not be solvable. (Imagine an automobile manufacturer trying to produce a 20 percent increase in sales in three months for $40,000!)

Problems do not exist in the abstract. They exist only when there is ownership. The owner might be a person, a group of people (such as the students in a class), an organization, or a country. A person may have ownership "assigned" by his or her supervisor in a company. That is, the company or the supervisor has ownership and assigns it to an employee or group of employees.

The idea of ownership is particularly important in teaching. If a student creates or helps create the problems to be solved, there is increased chance that the student will have ownership. Such ownership contributes to intrinsic motivation—a willingness to commit one's time and energies to solving the problem.

The type of ownership that comes from a student developing a problem that he or she really wants to solve is quite a bit different from the type of ownership that often occurs in school settings. When faced by a problem presented or assigned by the teacher or the textbook, a student may well translate this into, "My problem is to do the assignment and get a good grade. I don't have any interest in the problem presented by the teacher or the textbook." A skilled teacher will help students develop projects containing challenging problems they really care about.

Many teachers use PBL within their repertoire of instructional techniques. Within PBL, students often have a choice of the project to be done (the problems to be addressed, the tasks to be accomplished), subject to general guidelines the teacher established. Thus, students have the opportunity to have an increased level of ownership in the project they are working on. Research on PBL indicates that this ownership environment can increase the intrinsic motivation of students.

Representations of a Problem

There are many different ways to represent a problem. A problem can be represented mentally (in your own mind), orally, in writing, on a computer, and by other means. Each type of representation has certain advantages and disadvantages.

From a personal or ownership point of view, you first become aware of a problem situation in your mind and body. You sense, feel, or come to understand that something is not the way you want it to be. You form a mental representation, a mental model, of the problem situation. This mental model may include images, sounds, smells, and feelings. You can carry on a conversation with yourself—inside your head—about the problem situation. You begin to (mentally) transform the problem situation into a well-defined problem.

Mental representations of problems are essential. You create and use them whenever you work on a problem. But problems can also be represented in other ways. For example, you might represent a problem with spoken words and gestures. This could be useful if you are seeking the help of another person in dealing with a problem. The spoken words and gestures are an oral and body language representation or model of the problem.

You might represent a problem using pencil and paper (a written model). You might use this method do this to communicate with another person or with yourself.

Moreover, writing and drawing are powerful aids to memory. Thus, they are a powerful aid to solving or helping to solve many different types of problems.

For example, you probably keep an address book or list of the names, addresses, and phone numbers of your friends. Perhaps it contains additional information, such as e-mail addresses, birthdays, names of your friends' children, and so on. You have learned that an address book (a type of auxiliary memory) is more reliable than your memory.

There are still other ways to represent problems. For example, the language and notation of mathematics are useful for representing and solving certain types of problems. Here is a math "word problem." Two connecting rooms are to be carpeted. One room is 16 feet by 24 feet, and the other room is 12 feet by 14 feet. A particular type of carpet costs $17.45 per square yard. How much will the carpeting cost for the two connecting rooms? Figure B3 provides a graphic representation of the problem.

FIGURE B.3

Two rooms to be carpeted.

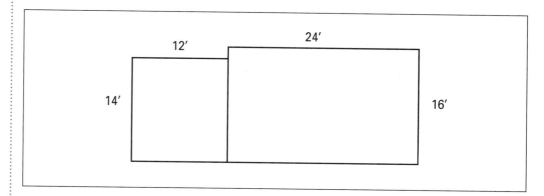

Conceptually, the problem is not too difficult. You can form a mental model draw the two rooms. Each room will be covered with carpet costing $17.45 per square yard. Thus, you need to figure out how many square yards you need for each room. Multiplying the number of square yards in a room by $17.45 gives the cost of the carpet for the room. Add the costs for the two rooms, and you have solved the problem.

Note that this is only one of the many possible ways to conceptualize this problem. You may well think of it in a different way.

The field of mathematics has produced the formula A = LW (Area equals Length times Width). Such a formula is an example of a mathematical model. It works for all rectangular shapes. Using the fact that there are 3 feet in a yard, the computation needed to solve this problem is:

Answer = $17.45 (16/3 x 24/3) + $17.45 (12/3 + 14/3)

Perhaps you can carry out this computation in your head. More likely, however, you will use pencil and paper, a calculator, or a computer.

There are two key ideas here. First, some of the problems people want to solve can be represented mathematically. Second, once a problem is represented as a math problem, much work still remains before the problem is solved. Over the past few thousand years, mathematicians have accumulated a great deal of knowledge about mathematics. Thus, if you can represent a problem as a math problem, you may be able to take advantage of the work that mathematicians have previously done. Mental artifacts, such as paper-and-pencil arithmetic, calculators, and computers, may be useful. Indeed, IT-based computational mathematics is now an important approach in representing and attempting to solve a wide range of mathematics problems.

A third key point has been completely ignored so far in this math problem example. Carpeting comes in various widths, with 12 feet being a common width. The carpet layer needs to figure out how many running feet of 12-feet-wide carpet will be needed. Cutting and "piecing" carpet is relatively time consuming. So, the carpet layer needs to figure out a carpet layout design that will involve a minimum of cutting and piecing. Note that the problem statement and the diagram do not indicate the thickness of the wall and the size of the doorway between the two rooms. Moreover, the statement of the problem did not indicate the relative locations of the two rooms. Do they share a wall in common and, if so, which wall?

In this short appendix it is not possible to further pursue the differences that tend to exist between "word problems" given in a math class and real-world problems of a somewhat similar nature. Suffices it to say that many students find considerable difficulty in transferring their school learning to solve the types of problems they encounter outside of school. Appropriately designed PBL can help overcome this difficulty.

Representing Problems Using Computers

One particularly important feature of a mental model is that it is easily changed. You can "think" a change. This allows you to quickly consider a number of different alternatives, both in how you might solve a problem and in identifying what problem you really want to solve. You can quickly pose and answer "what if?" types of questions about possible alternative actions you might take.

Other representations, such as through writing and mathematics, are useful because they are a supplement to your brain. Written representations of problems facilitate sharing with yourself and others over time and distance. However, a written model is not as easily changed as a mental model. The written word has a permanency that is desirable in some situations, but is a difficulty in others. You cannot merely "think" a change. Erasing is messy. And, if you happen to be writing with a ball-point pen, erasing is nearly impossible.

When a problem is represented with a computer, we call this a *computer model* or a *computer representation* of the problem. For some problems, a computer model has some of the same characteristics as a mental model. Some computer models are easy to change and allow easy exploration of alternatives.

For example, suppose the problem you face (that is, the task you want to accomplish) involves writing a report on some work you have done. You write using a word processor. Thus, you produce a computer model of the report. You know, of course, that a key to high-quality writing is "revise, revise, revise." This is much more easily done with a computer model of a report than it is with a paper-and-pencil model of a report. In addition, a computer can assist in spell checking and grammar checking, and it can be used to produce a nicely formatted final product.

In the representation of problems, computers are useful in some cases and not at all useful in others. For example, a computer can easily present data in a variety of graphical formats, such as line graph or bar graph, or in the form of graphs of two- and three-dimensional mathematical functions.

But a computer may not be a good substitute for the doodling and similar types of graphical mind-mapping activities that many people use when attacking problems. Suppose that one's mental representation of a problem is in terms of analogy, metaphor, mental pictures, smells, and so on. Research that has delved into the inner workings of the minds of successful researchers and inventors suggests that these representations are common and perhaps necessary. A computer may be of little use in manipulating such a mental representation.

Problem Posing and Clarification

Many of the things that people call problems are actually poorly defined problem situations. In this case, one or more of the four components of a clearly defined problem are missing. For example, suppose you turn on a television set and view a brief news item about the homeless people in a large city and the starving children in a foreign nation. The announcer continues with a news item about students in our schools scoring poorly on an international test, relative to those from some other countries. The announcer presents each news item as a major problem. But, are these really clearly defined problems?

You can ask yourself four questions:

1. Is there a clearly defined given initial situation? (Do I really know the facts? Can I check out the facts through alternative sources that I feel are reliable?)

2. Is there a clearly defined goal? (Is it really clear to me how I would like things to be? Are there a number of possible goals? Which goal or goals seem most feasible and viable? Will I be able to tell if the goal has been achieved?)

3. Do I know what resources are available to me that I could use to help achieve the goal? In addition, are there rules, regulations, and guidelines I need to know about as I work to solve this problem?

4. Do I have ownership—do I care enough to devote some of my own resources? (Am I willing to spend some of my own time, money, and psychic energy on achieving the goal?)

If you can answer "yes" to each of these questions, then you (personally) have a formal, clearly defined problem.

Often, your answer to one or more of the questions will be "no." Then, the last question is crucial. If you have ownership—if you really care about the situation—you may begin to think about it. You may decide on what you feel are appropriate statements of the givens and the goal. You may seek resources from others and make a commitment of your own resources. You may then proceed to attempt to solve the problem.

The process of creating a clearly defined problem is called *problem posing* or *problem clarification*. It usually proceeds in two phases. First, your mind or body senses or is made aware of a problem situation. You decide that the problem situation interests you—you have some ownership. Second, you begin to work on clarifying the givens, the goal, and the resources. Perhaps you consider alternative goals and sense which would contribute most to your ownership of the problem situation.

Identifying and posing problem situations and then transforming them into well-defined problems are higher-order thinking tasks. These tasks are not adequately addressed in our educational system. To a very large extent, students are asked to work on problems posed by the teacher and/or the curriculum materials. The problems tend to be quite limited in scope and typically lack a real-world quality. Typically, students are not asked to explore problem situations such as hunger, homelessness, prejudice, terrorism, and so on. They tend to (incorrectly) "learn" that all problems have solutions, and that they are "dumb" or not working hard enough if they do not find "the solution" to an assigned problem.

The result of the problem-posing process is a problem that is sufficiently well defined so that you can begin to work on solving it. As you work on the problem, you will likely develop a still better understanding of it. You may redefine the goal and/or come to understand the goal better. You may come to understand the given initial situation better;

indeed, you may decide to do some research to gain more information about it. Problem posing is an ongoing process as you work to understand and solve a problem.

Problem posing is a higher-order thinking skill that is an integral component of every domain. Moreover, it is a component of problem solving that cuts across all discipline areas. Some additional general-purpose problem-solving ideas are given in the next two sections.

Some Problem-Solving Strategies

A strategy can be thought of as a plan, a heuristic, a rule of thumb, a possible way to approach the solving of some type of problem. For example, perhaps one of the problems that you have to deal with is finding a parking place at work or at school. If so, you have probably developed a strategy, for example, a particular time of day when you look for a parking place or use a particular search pattern. Your strategy may not always be successful, but you find it useful.

Every problem-solving domain has its own strategies. Research suggests the following:

1. There are relatively few strategies that are powerful and applicable across all domains. (Breaking a big problem into smaller problems is one of these general-purpose strategies. Doing library research is another general-purpose strategy.) Because each subject matter (each domain) has its own set of domain-specific problem-solving strategies, one needs to know a great deal about a particular domain and its problem-solving strategies to be good at solving problems within that domain.

2. The typical person has few explicit strategies in any particular domain. This suggests that if we help a person gain a few more domain-specific strategies, it might make a significant difference in overall problem-solving performance in that domain. It also suggests the value of helping students to learn strategies that cut across many different domains.

The idea of breaking big problems into smaller problems is called the top-down strategy. The idea is that it may be far easier to deal with a number of small problems than it is to deal with one large problem. For example, the task of writing a long document may be approached by developing an outline, and then writing small pieces that fill in details on the outline.

Library research is a type of "ask an expert" strategy. A large library contains the accumulated expertise of thousands of experts. The Web is a rapidly expanding global library. It is not easy to become skilled at searching the Web. For example, are you skilled in using the Web to find information that will help you in dealing with language arts problems, math problems, science problems, social science problems, personal problems, health problems, entertainment problems, and so on? Each domain presents its own information retrieval challenges.

An alternative to using a library in an "ask an expert" approach is to actually ask a human expert. Many people make their livings by being consultants. They consider themselves to be experts within their own specific domains, and they get paid for answering questions and solving problems within their areas of expertise. For example, the Ask ERIC system provides a human interface (free consulting) to the ERIC information retrieval system (AskERIC).

The various fields of science share a common strategy called the scientific method. It consists of posing and testing hypotheses. This is a form of problem posing and problem solving. Scientists work to carefully define a problem or problem area they are exploring. They want to be able to communicate the problem to others, both now and in the future. They want to do work that others can build upon. Well-done scientific research (that is, well-done problem solving in science) contributes to the accumulated knowledge in the field.

You have lots of domain-specific strategies. Think about some of the strategies you have for making friends, for learning, for getting to work on time, for finding things you have misplaced, and so on. Many of your strategies are so ingrained that you use them automatically—without conscious thought. You may even use them when they are ineffective.

The use of ineffective strategies is common. For example, how do you memorize a set of materials? Do you just read the materials over and over again? This is not a very effective strategy. There are many memorization strategies that are better. A useful and simple strategy is pausing to review. Other strategies include finding familiar chunks, identifying patterns, and building associations between what you are memorizing and things that are familiar to you.

Some learners are good at inventing strategies that are effective for themselves. Most learners can benefit greatly from some help in identifying and learning appropriate strategies. In general, a person who is a good teacher in a particular domain is good at helping students recognize, learn, and fully internalize effective strategies in that domain. Often this requires that a student unlearn previously acquired strategies or habits.

Problem-solving strategies can be a lesson topic within any subject you teach. Individually and collectively your students can develop and study the strategies they and others use in learning the subject content area and learning to solve the problems in the subject area. A whole-class IT-assisted PBL project in a course might be to develop and desktop publish a book of strategies that will be useful to students who will take the course in the future.

A General Strategy for Problem Solving

Here is a general six-step strategy you can follow in attempting to solve almost any problem. This six-step strategy is a modification of ideas discussed in Polya (1957) and can be called the Polya Strategy or the Six-Step Strategy. Note that there is no guarantee that use of the Six-Step Strategy will lead to success in solving a particular problem. You may lack the knowledge, skills, time, and other resources needed to solve a particular problem, or the problem might not be solvable.

1. **Understand the problem.** Among other things, this includes working toward having a clearly defined problem. You need an initial understanding of the givens, resources, and goal. This requires knowledge of the domains of the problem, which could well be interdisciplinary.

2. **Determine a plan of action.** This is a thinking activity. What strategies will you apply? What resources will you use, how will you use them, in what order will you use them? Are the resources adequate to the task?

3. **Think carefully about possible consequences of carrying out your plan of action.** Place major emphasis on trying to anticipate undesirable outcomes. What new problems will be created? You may decide to stop working on the problem or return to Step 1 as a consequence of this thinking.

4. Carry out your plan of action. Do so in a thoughtful manner. This thinking may lead you to the conclusion that you need to return to one of the earlier steps. Note that this reflective thinking leads to increased expertise.

5. Check to see if the desired goal has been achieved by carrying out your plan of action. Then do one of the following:

   A. If the problem has been solved, go to Step 6.

   B. If the problem has not been solved and you are willing to devote more time and energy to it, use the knowledge and experience you have gained as you return to Step 1 or Step 2.

   C. Make a decision to stop working on the problem. This might be a temporary or a permanent decision. Keep in mind that the problem you are working on may not be solvable, or it may be beyond your current capabilities and resources.

6. Do a careful analysis of the steps you have carried out and the results you have achieved to see if you have created new, additional problems that need to be addressed. Reflect on what you have learned by solving the problem. Think about how your increased knowledge and skills can be used in other problem-solving situations. (Work to increase your reflective intelligence!)

Many people have found that this Six-Step Strategy for problem solving is worth memorizing. As a teacher, you might decide that one of your goals in teaching problem solving is to have all your students memorize this strategy and practice it so that it becomes second nature. Students will need to practice it in many different domains in order to help increase transfer of learning. This will help to increase your students' expertise in solving problems.

Many of the steps in this Six-Step Strategy require careful thinking. However, there are a steadily growing number of situations in which much of the work of Step 4 can be carried out by a computer. The person who is skilled at using a computer for this purpose may gain a significant advantage in problem solving, as compared to a person who lacks computer knowledge and skill.

Working toward Increased Expertise

One of the goals of instruction in any subject area is to help students increase their expertise at posing, representing, and solving problems in the subject area. People can get better at whatever they do. A person can get better at a sport, at a hobby or craft, or in an academic field. A person's level of expertise can increase through learning and practice. A person who is really good at something relative to his or her peers is considered to be an expert.

It is important to distinguish between having some level of expertise and being an expert. The word *expertise* does not mean any particular level of ability. For anything you can do, you can imagine a scale of performance that runs from very low expertise to very high expertise (see Figure B.4). When a person has a high level of expertise in some particular area, we call this person an expert. Bereiter and Scardamalia (1993) provide an excellent summary of research about expertise.

FIGURE B.4

An "expertise" scale.

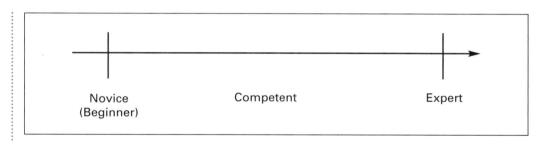

Novice (Beginner)   Competent   Expert

Research on expertise indicates that it takes many years of study, practice, and hard work for individuals to achieve their full potential in any particular area of expertise. For example, consider any one of the eight areas of intelligence identified by Howard Gardner. If a person is naturally talented in one of these areas and works really hard for 10 to 15 years within that specific area, that person is apt to achieve world-class status in that area. It is a combination of talent and hard work over many years (nature and nurture) that allows a person to achieve a high level of expertise in an area.

Because it takes so much time and effort to achieve a high level of expertise in just one narrow field, few people achieve a high level of expertise in multiple fields. For example, consider how few professional athletes perform at a world class level in two different sports, or consider the number of general practitioner versus the number of specialists in medicine.

One of the successes in the field of artificial intelligence has been the development of *expert systems,* which are computer programs that exhibit a considerable level of expertise in solving problems within a specific (typically, very narrow) domain. In a number of narrowly defined domains, expert systems or humans working together with an expert system can perform at a quite high level of expertise. This, of course, has profound implications in education. Suppose a computer program (an expert system) exists with a specific domain that is being covered in a school curriculum. Now, what do we want students to learn about solving problems in that domain? Do we want students to learn to compete with the expert system, or learn to work with the expert system?

You may think that such questions do not pertain to our ordinary curriculum. However, one can think of a handheld calculator as having some artificial intelligence. More sophisticated calculators can solve a wide range of math problems. A spelling checker in a word processor has a certain level of expertise, as does a grammar checker. The point is that progress in artificial intelligence is providing us with powerful aids to problem solving (that is, resources) in many different domains.

Transfer of Learning

Transfer of learning deals with transferring one's knowledge and skills from one problem-solving situation to another. You need to know about transfer of learning in order to help increase the transfer of learning your students achieve.

Transfer of learning is commonplace and often done without conscious thought. For example, suppose that when you were a child and learning to tie your shoes, all of your shoes had brown cotton shoelaces. You mastered tying brown cotton shoelaces. The next year you got new shoes. The new shoes were a little bigger, and they had white nylon shoe laces. The chances are that you had no trouble whatsoever in transferring your shoe-tying skills to the new larger shoes with the different shoelaces.

However, there are many transfer-of-learning situations that are far more difficult. For example, a secondary school math class might teach the metric system of units. From the math class, students go to a science class. Frequently the science teacher reports that the students claim a complete lack of knowledge about the metric system. Essentially no transfer of learning has occurred from the math class to the science class.

The goal of gaining general skills in the transfer of your learning is easier said than done. Researchers have worked to develop a general theory of transfer of learning—a theory that could help students get better at transfer. This has proven to be a difficult research problem.

At one time, it was common to talk about transfer of learning in terms of near and far transfer. This theory of transfer suggested that some problems and tasks are so nearly alike that transfer of learning occurs easily and naturally. This is called *near transfer*. The previously described shoe tying example illustrates near transfer. Other problems and tasks required more concentrated effort and thinking for transfer to occur. This is called *far transfer.*

The theory of near and far transfer does not help us much in our teaching. We know that near and far transfer occur. But, what is "near" or "far" varies with the person attempting to do the transfer. We know that far transfer does not readily occur for most students. The difficulty with this theory of near and far transfer is that it does not provide a foundation or a plan for helping a person to get better at transfer.

In recent years, the low-road/high-road theory on transfer of learning, developed by Salomon and Perkins (1988), has proven to be more fruitful. Low-road transfer refers to developing some knowledge or skill to a high level of automaticity. It usually requires a great deal of practice in varying settings. Shoe tying, keyboarding, steering a car, and one-digit arithmetic facts are examples of areas in which such automaticity can be achieved and is quite useful.

On the other hand, high-road transfer involves cognitive understanding, purposeful and conscious analysis, mindfulness, and application of strategies that cut across disciplines. In high-road transfer, there is deliberate mindful abstraction of the idea that can transfer, and then conscious and deliberate application of the idea when faced by a problem where the idea may be useful.

For example, consider the top-down strategy of breaking a big problem into smaller components. You can learn the name and learn the concept of this strategy. You can practice this strategy in many different domains. You can reflect on the strategy and how it fits you and your way of dealing with the problems you encounter. Similar comments hold for the library research strategy.

Eventually, you can incorporate a strategy into your repertoire of approaches to problem solving. When you encounter a new problem that is not solved by low-road transfer, you begin to mentally run through your list of strategies useful in high-road transfer. You may decide that breaking the problem into smaller pieces would be an effective strategy to apply, or you may decide that library research (a Web search) is a good starting point.

Two keys to high-road transfer are mindfulness and reflectiveness. View every problem-solving situation as an opportunity to learn. After solving a problem, reflect about what you have learned about problem solving by solving the problem. Be mindful of ideas that are of potential use in solving other problems. Similar reflection can profitably be applied to saturations in which you fail to solve a problem.

Of course, there is a wide range of problems that lie between those easily handled by low-road transfer and those that require the careful, conscious, well-reasoned, mindful approaches suggested by high-road transfer. Previously in this appendix it was mentioned that many years of hard work are required to gain a high level of expertise in a domain. To a large extent, this work results in moving many problems from the middle ground in the domain toward the low-road transfer end of the scale. More and more of the problems you encounter in the domain are quickly and easily solved, almost without conscious thought and effort.

PBL and Problem Solving

PBL is an individual or group activity that goes on over a period of time, resulting in a product, presentation, or performance. PBL typically has a timeline, milestones, and other aspects of formative evaluation as the project proceeds.

Doing a project and solving a problem have much in common. For example, in PBL a student or team of students typically has considerable latitude in posing the details of what will be accomplished in the project. There are limited resources, such as time. There is a clear goal of a product, presentation, or performance. The student or team of students may well develop a high level of ownership as work on the project progresses. Thus, any PBL environment is a good environment for teaching problem solving.

PBL shares much in common with process writing. In the United States, the roots of process writing are often traced back to the Bay Area Writing Project, which began about 1975. A six-step version of process writing is:

1. brainstorming
2. organizing the brainstormed ideas
3. developing a draft
4. obtaining feedback
5. revising, which may involve going back to earlier steps
6. publishing

This list can be viewed as a process writing strategy for accomplishing the task (solving the problem) of doing a writing project.

Summary of Important Ideas

Each classroom teaching situation provides an environment that can be used to help students improve their problem-solving and higher-order thinking skills. Students will make significant progress if:

1. They have ownership of the problems to be solved and the tasks to be accomplished. They are intrinsically motivated.

2. The problems to be solve and the tasks to be accomplished are challenging—they stretch the capabilities of the students.

3. There is explicit instruction on key ideas such as:

   A. Problem posing. Working to achieve a clearly defined problem. As you work to solve a problem, continue to spend time working to define the problem.

   B. Problem representation.

   C. Building on your own previous work and on the work of others.

D. Transfer of learning.

E. Viewing each problem or project as a learning opportunity. As you work on solving a problem try to learn things that will help you in the future. Practice metacognition. Do a conscious, considered analysis of the components and the overall process in each challenging problem that you address. This will help you to get better at solving problems.

F. The roles of IT in problem solving.

references and resources

The references and resources cited in this section are drawn from Dave Moursund's PBL Web site at http://darkwing.uoregon. edu/~moursund/PBL/. The references listed on that Web site are regularly checked for broken links and are updated as new materials are identified.

Applied Measurement in Education. (1992). [Special issue]. 4(4).

This journal issue provides an in-depth analysis of the nature of, practices in, and concerns about performance assessment. The articles not only discuss the difference between the new and traditional approaches to student assessment, but they also define performance assessment, authentic assessment, and portfolio assessment.

Armstrong, Sara. (2002). *The key learning community: Cultivating "multiple intelligences."* [Online]. Accessed 5/28/02: **http://glef.org/keylearning.html**

This article describes a public K–11 school in Indianapolis, Indiana, where PBL is used extensively. PBL is implemented in a teaching and learning environment focusing on multiple intelligences.

AskERIC. [Online]. Accessed 5/28/02: **www.askeric.org**

Quoting from the Web site: "ERIC is the Educational Resources Information Center (ERIC), a federally funded national information system that provides, through its 16 subject-specific clearinghouses, associated adjunct clearinghouses, and support components, a variety of services and products on a broad range of education-related issues...."

"Need to know the latest information on special education, curriculum development, or other education topics? Just AskERIC! When you submit your education question to AskERIC Q&A, you'll receive a personal e-mail response within two business days from one of the network information specialists in the ERIC system! We will send you a list of ERIC database citations that deal with your topic and will also refer you to other Internet resources for additional information. It's that easy."

Awesome Library: Assessment Information. [Online]. Accessed 5/28/02:
**www.awesomelibrary.org/Office/Teacher/Assessment_Information/
Assessment_Information.html**

> This Web site was originally developed through federal grants. It is an excellent site, covering a wide range of educational topics. The specific address given for the site focuses on authentic assessment, portfolios, program evaluation, rubrics, and school report cards.

Barrett, H.C. (1994). Technology-supported assessment portfolios. *The Computing Teacher, 21*(6), 9–12.

> Barrett examines a number of different pieces of software, as well as some hardware, used in electronic portfolios and other aspects of student assessment.

Bereiter, C., & Scardamalia, M. (1993). *Surpassing ourselves: An inquiry into the nature and implications of expertise.* Chicago, IL: Open Court.

> This is a seminal book on expertise. It is aimed at educators and education in general, but it also discusses some of the roles computers play in expertise. It describes ways to help people gain increased expertise and contains an extensive bibliography.

Blumenfeld, P. C., Soloway, S., Marx, R. W., Krajcik, J. S., Guzdial, M., & Palincsar, A. (1991). Motivating project-based learning: Sustaining the doing, supporting the learning. *Educational Psychologist, 26*(3–4), 369–398.

> This extensive article is based on research going on at the University of Michigan. It provides an excellent summary of the research on PBL at the precollege level. It has a substantial focus on uses of computers and other IT in PBL.

Boone, R. (Ed.). (1991). *Teaching process writing with computers.* Eugene, OR: International Society for Technology in Education.

> This book provides a good summary of the research literature and practical aspects of using computers in process writing.

Breivik, P.S., & Senn, J.A. (1994). *Information literacy: Educating children for the 21st century.* New York: Scholastic.

> This book provides an in-depth discussion of the concept of information literacy: what it is and how to implement it in schools through collaboration between classroom teachers and media center specialists.

Brewer, R. (1996). *Exemplars: A teacher's solution.* Underhill, VT: Exemplars.

> Vermont has made a major commitment to authentic assessment in its schools. This book includes a number of examples of rubrics used in authentic assessment.

Brookhart, Susan M. (1999). The art and science of classroom assessment: The missing part of pedagogy. *ERIC Digest.* [Online]. Accessed 5/28/02:
www.ed.gov/databases/ERIC_Digests/ed432938.html

> Quoting from the Web site: "'Assessment' means to gather and interpret information about students' achievement, and 'achievement' means the level of attainment of learning goals of college courses. Assessing students' achievement is generally accomplished through tests, classroom and take-home assignments, and assigned projects. Strictly speaking, 'assessment' refers to assignments and tasks that provide information, and 'evaluation' refers to judgments based on that information...."

"Information from classroom assessments—grades, scores, and judgments about students' work resulting from tests, assignments, projects, and other work—must be meaningful and accurate (that is, valid and reliable). The results of assessment should be indicators of the particular learning goals for the course, measuring those goals in proportion to their emphasis in the course. An instructor should be confident that students' scores accurately represent their level of achievement. *The Art and Science of Classroom Assessment* describes five different kinds of learning goals or 'achievement targets': knowledge of facts and concepts (recall); thinking, reasoning, and problem solving using one's knowledge; skill in procedures or processes, such as using a microscope; constructing projects, reports, artwork, or other products; and dispositions, such as appreciating the importance of a discipline. Different methods of assessment are better suited for measuring different kinds of achievement."

Case Studies in Science. [Online]. Accessed 5/28/02:
http://ublib.buffalo.edu/libraries/projects/cases/webcase.htm

This site's main focus is on problem-based learning in college courses. Links to a number of case study examples are provided in business, dentistry, engineering, engineering ethics, medicine, pharmacy, public policy, science, science ethics, and sociology.

Center for Problem-Based Learning. [Online]. Accessed 5/28/02:
www.imsa.edu/team/cpbl/cpbl.html

This is an excellent source of information on problem-based learning. Quoting from the Web site: "The Center for Problem-Based Learning was created by the Illinois Science and Mathematics Academy to engage in PBL research, information exchange, teacher training and curriculum development in K–16 educational settings."

The Computing Teacher. (1994, March). [Special issue].

This theme issue is devoted to alternative assessment.

Concord Consortium. [Online]. Accessed 5/28/02: **www.concord.org/projects/**

The Projects link on the home page points to a large list of current and past projects this organization has carried out. Many have been of nationwide or worldwide scope, and they provide excellent examples of PBL at its best.

Conference on English Education (CEE). [Online]. Accessed 5/28/02:
www.ncte.org/cee/

The Conference on English Education (CEE) is made up of an active constituency concerned with the process of educating teachers of English, reading, and language arts. Formed in 1963, CEE focuses on both preservice training and inservice development of teachers. A committee within CEE focuses on IT in English education.

Cooperative Learning Center at University of Minnesota. [Online]. Accessed 5/28/02:
www.clcrc.com

Quoting from the Web site: "Cooperative Learning is a relationship in a group of students that requires positive interdependence (a sense of sink or swim together), individual accountability (each of us has to contribute and learn), interpersonal skills (communication, trust, leadership, decision making, and conflict resolution), face-to-face promotive interaction, and processing (reflecting on how well the team is functioning and how to function even better)."

CORD: Project-Based Learning [Online]. Accessed 5/28/02:
www.cord.org/lev2.cfm/65/

Quoting from the Web site: "Project-based learning is a teaching and learning strategy that engages students in complex activities. It usually requires several steps and some duration—more than a couple of class days and up to a semester—and cooperative group learning. Projects may focus on the development of a product or performance, and they generally call upon students to organize their activities, conduct research, solve problems, and synthesize information. Projects are often interdisciplinary. For example, a project in which students draft plans for and build a structure, investigate its environmental impact, document the building process, and develop spreadsheets for the associated accounting would involve the use of skills and concepts drawn from courses in English, mathematics, building trades, drafting and/or design, and biology. Although projects as a methodology are not a new concept; it is an approach that supports the many tasks facing teachers today, such as meeting state standards, incorporating authentic assessment, infusing higher-order thinking skills, guiding students in life choices, and providing experiences that tap individual student interests and abilities. Furthermore, the student products created during projects provide the means by which teachers can include authentic assessment in their instruction."

D'Ignazio, F. (1995–97). Multimedia sandbox. [Column]. *Learning & Leading with Technology.* Eugene, OR: International Society for Technology in Education.

This continuing series of articles explores a wide range of multimedia projects that can be used in the classroom. In addition, there is a focus on free and inexpensive pieces of equipment that can be used in developing multimedia projects. D'Ignazio places major emphasis on making do with whatever hardware and software is available.

Distance Learning. [Online]. Accessed 5/28/02:
http://otec.uoregon.edu/distance_learning.htm

Faculty members may be interested in carrying out some or all aspects of a PBL lesson via distance learning. This distance learning Web site provides a good introduction to the field.

Educational Leadership. (1992). [Special issue]. 49(8).

This issue of *Educational Leadership* provides an in-depth analysis of the nature of, practices in, and concerns about performance assessment. The articles not only discuss the difference between the new and traditional approaches to student assessment, but they also define performance assessment, authentic assessment, and portfolio assessment.

Educational Leadership. (1997, September). [Special issue].

This theme issue of Educational Leadership focuses specifically on teaching for multiple intelligences. It contains 16 articles addressing various aspects of Howard Gardner's theory of multiple intelligences and their applications in the classroom. It includes an article written by Gardner and an interview with him. Gardner's ideas are being widely implemented in education, both in the United States and in other countries.

Federal Resources for Educational Excellence (FREE). [Online]. Accessed 5/28/02: **www.ed.gov/free/**

> This Web site contains links to a huge number of solid sources of information that students can use as they design and carry out projects.

Fogarty, R. (Ed.). (1996). *Student portfolios: A collection of articles.* Palatine, IL: IRI/Skylight Training and Publishing.

> Major sections of this book address the following topics: choosing portfolios, using portfolios, and perusing portfolios. Two articles focus on electronic portfolios and one addresses self-assessment.

Fosnot, C. T. (Ed.). (1996). *Constructivism: Theory, perspectives, and practice.* New York: Teachers College, Columbia University.

> This book is a collection of research and practice-based articles that explore the theory and practice of constructivism.

Frensch, P., & Funke, J. (Eds.). (1995). *Complex problem solving: The European perspective.* Hillsdale, NJ: Lawrence Erlbaum Associates.

> This book provides an excellent overview of the current research on complex problem solving. The main emphasis is on research being done in Europe. However, there is an excellent chapter written by Robert Sternberg that compares and contrasts problem-solving research in the United States with problem-solving research in Europe. In recent years, much of the problem-solving research in the United States has focused on specific domains in which one can acquire a great deal of expertise. Examples include chess, electronics, legal reasoning, physics, and writing. Research in Europe tends to focus on more general problems, such as managing the resources of a city. Europeans also use complex computer simulations of the problem-solving environments to be studied.

Gardner, H. (1983). *Frames of mind: The theory of multiple intelligences.* New York: Basic Books.

> A new edition of this book was published in 1993, which contains additional material in the preface. The book is written for a somewhat narrow, technical audience but has proved to be immensely popular, as have the general ideas contained in the book. This book and *Multiple Intelligences* (see the next entry) provide an excellent introduction to the theory and applications of multiple intelligences.

Gardner, H. (1993). *Multiple intelligences: The theory in practice.* New York: Basic Books.

> This book expands on ideas originally presented in *Frames of Mind* (see previous entry). It provides a variety of examples of applications of the original theory. There is considerable emphasis on applications in education.

Glasgow, N. A. (1997). *New curriculum for new times: A guide to student-centered problem-based learning.* Thousand Oaks, CA: Corwin Press.

> Neal Glasgow is a secondary school teacher writing about the way he teaches. Problem-based learning is PBL in which the focus is on a specific problem to be solved or task to be accomplished. Glasgow analyzes the advantages of problem-based learning and the challenges a teacher faces in implementing problem-based learning. This book is an excellent testimonial and "how to do it" book on PBL.

Goldman, D. (1995). *Emotional intelligence.* New York: Bantam Books.

Emotions are a critical component of the makeup of people. Goldman's book summarizes and analyzes the research on how a person's emotional "intelligence" contributes to that person's functioning well in society. He points out that in many situations, emotional intelligence is a better predictor of success in solving problems and accomplishing tasks than are traditional measures of IQ.

Harrington, Thomas F. (1995). Assessment of abilities. *ERIC Digest* [Online]. Accessed 5/28/02: **www.ed.gov/databases/ERIC_Digests/ed389960.html**

Quoting from the Web site: "ABSTRACT—This digest recommends assessing all of a person's abilities, not just some. It also discusses self-report in the context of ability assessment. Current use of self-assessment methodology taps more ability areas than existing ability or aptitude tests cover. Alternative testing approaches have been called for which enhance self-discovery and awareness. Some recent self-report studies show at least comparable validity with more traditional approaches. Some researchers are advocating the self-assessment methodology, which can substantially cut loss of instructional time and cost, evaluate hard-to-assess constructs, and deliver information most people feel is useful for self-knowledge and career planning. Philosophically, the process of self-evaluation fits the belief that individuals are in the best position to assess since they have access to a large data base on their own successes and failures in their abilities. Most misgivings about the methodology seem to center around beliefs that individuals have a tendency to be lenient and are not objective enough in their self-analysis to provide accurate self-reports. Contains 11 references."

Helgeson, S.L. (1992). *Problem solving research in middle/junior high school science education.* Columbus, OH: ERIC Clearinghouse for Mathematics, Science, and Environmental Education.

This is an extremely detailed literature review of research on problem solving. It highlights both the possibilities and difficulties of improving higher-order thinking.

International Society for Technology in Education. (1998). *National Educational Technology Standards for Students.* Eugene, OR: Author.

The International Society for Technology in Education (ISTE) is a nonprofit professional society of educators working to improve education through appropriate use of IT. ISTE's main emphasis is on K–12 education and teacher education. Information about ISTE products, services, and membership is given on the ISTE Web site at http://www.iste.org/. The Technology Standards document resulted from the first phase of a multiyear project to develop IT standards for students at the pre-K–12 grade levels. The complete document is available as a PDF file on the ISTE Web site at www.iste.org.

An Introduction to Problem-Based Learning: Bison, Brucella, and DNA Research in Greater Yellowstone. [Online]. Accessed 5/28/02: **www.icsrc.org/TILT/bison/resources/Pbl.htm**

This Web site contains a good, brief introduction to PBL It includes some examples and some useful links.

Quoting from the Web site: "Finkle and Torp (1995) state that 'problem-based learning is a curriculum development and instructional system that simultaneously develops both problem-solving strategies and disciplinary knowledge bases and skills by placing students in the active role of problem solvers confronted with an ill-structured problem that mirrors real-world problems.'"

Johnson, D.W., & Johnson, R.T. (1989). Social skills for successful group work. *Educational Leadership, 47*(4), 29–33.

Johnson and Johnson are international leaders in cooperative learning. This article makes a case for teaching communication skills as preparation for cooperative learning.

Johnson, R.T. (1986). Comparison of computer-assisted cooperative, competitive, and individualistic learning. *American Educational Research Journal, 23*(3), 382–392.

In this study, computer-assisted cooperative learning was found to be superior in terms of promoting achievement, problem solving, interaction, and the perceived status of female students.

Kehoe, Colleen, & Guzdial, Mark. (1997). *What we know about technological support for project-based learning.* [Online]. Accessed 5/28/02: **www.cc.gatech.edu/grads/k/Colleen.Kehoe/papers/stable/fie.html**

Quoting the abstract and first paragraph from the Web site: "Abstract. This paper describes our experiences in building tools to support project-based learning. We briefly describe our successes and failures in three areas: team management and collaboration, supporting reflection, and providing information in project-based form. Our approach combines insights on learning from cognitive science with an appreciation for the practical challenges raised by focusing on projects in a class. Based on our experiences, we conclude that technology can play an important role in supporting project-based learning...."

"Much of engineering education focuses on projects used to enhance students' learning of engineering practice and relevant concepts of science and engineering. Without projects, engineering education can become too focused on abstract concepts without students' understanding of related concepts and how to apply the concepts [1]. Further, research in cognitive science suggests that learning outside of an applicable situation can lead to brittle or inert knowledge, that is, knowledge that does not get transferred to new problems and new situations [2]."

Kulik, J. A. (1994). Meta-analytic studies of findings on computer-based instruction. In E. Baker & H. O'Neill (Eds.), *Technology assessment in education and training* (pp. 9–33). Hillsdale, NJ: Lawrence Erlbaum Associates.

James Kulik has been doing metastudies on computer-based learning (computer-assisted learning) for many years. A number of his studies have been funded by the National Science Foundation and other federal agencies. This article analyzes of the metastudies he and others have carried out—that is, it is a meta-metastudy. It presents convincing evidence that CAL works. The article also contains an extensive bibliography, so it provides an excellent starting point for exploring the literature on CAL.

Lave, J., & Wenger, E. (1991). *Situated learning: Legitimate peripheral participation.* Cambridge University Press.

Publisher's note. "In this important theoretical treatise, Jean Lave, anthropologist, and Etienne Wenger, computer scientist, push forward the notion of situated learning—that learning is fundamentally a social process and not solely in the learner's head. The authors maintain that learning viewed as situated activity has as its central defining characteristic a process they call legitimate peripheral participation. Learners participate in communities of practitioners, moving toward full participation in the sociocultural practices of a community. Legitimate peripheral participation provides a way to speak about crucial relations between newcomers and oldtimers and about their activities, identities, artifacts, knowledge, and practice. The communities discussed in the book are midwives, tailors, quartermasters, butchers, and recovering alcoholics; however, the process by which participants in those communities learn can be generalized to other social groups.

Leadership Institute Integrating Internet, Instruction, and Curriculum. [Online]. Accessed 5/28/02: **www.ed.fnal.gov/trc/projects/hs_proj.html**

This Web site contains a number of examples of projects suitable for use at various grade levels. They were designed to demonstrate principles of engaged learning and effective use of technology by K–12 teachers who participated in staff development programs at Fermi National Accelerator Laboratory, a U.S. Department of Energy National Laboratory in Batavia, Illinois.

Maryland Virtual High School of Science and Mathematics. [Online]. Accessed 5/28/02: **http://mvhs1.mbhs.edu**

This virtual high school involves students from many campuses. Much of the "classwork" can be classified as problem-based learning, and the PBL routinely makes use of powerful computer hardware and software.

Quoting from the Web site: "Preparing students to 'do' science in the real world of the future means guiding them in 'doing' science now. The Maryland Virtual High School of Science and Mathematics entails bringing to the classroom the same team problem-solving, technology-rich approaches currently used in research and business. Computational science has become a powerful paradigm to complement other approaches. Computational tools, ranging from spreadsheets on microprocessors to advanced molecular modeling tools on supercomputers, are allowing scientists to model processes too costly or impossible to investigate in other ways."

Meng, E., & Doran, R.L. (1993). *Improving instruction and learning through evaluation: Elementary school science.* Columbus, OH: ERIC.

This work explores many different ways to assess elementary school science. The emphasis is on assessment aligned with a philosophy of hands-on science instruction.

Moursund, D. G. (1996, 2001). *Increasing your expertise as a problem solver: Some roles of computers.* [Online]. Accessed 5/28/02: **http://darkwing.uoregon.edu/~moursund/PSBook1996/index.htm**

This is a revised edition of a full-length book that was originally published by the International Society for Technology in Education. It is intended mainly for teachers and for teachers of teachers. There is a strong parallel between doing a project and solving a problem. And, or course, problem-based learning is closely related to both PBL and problem solving.

Moursund, D. G. (1997). *The future of information technology in education.* [Online]. Accessed 5/28/02: **http://darkwing.uoregon.edu/~moursund/FuturesBook1997/**

A number of different forecasting techniques are used in analyzing and predicting the future of IT in education. While the primary focus is on education at the K–12 level in the United States, the book also includes some information on postsecondary education and educational systems throughout the world.

Moursund, D. G. (2002). *Workshop on IT-Assisted Project-Based Learning.* [Online]. Accessed 5/28/02: **http://darkwing.uoregon.edu/~moursund/PBL/**

This Web site includes an extensive syllabus for a workshop or short course on PBL.

My Design Primer. [Online]. Accessed 5/28/02: **www.mydesignprimer.com/index.html**

Quoting from the Web site: "Design Studio is a company that focuses on producing effective communication and marketing materials while maintaining personal client relationships. We believe that, by communicating effectively with our clients, we can understand their goals and they can make the best choices for their needs and budgets. This site was created to assist our clients and others in understanding the often confusing terms and ideas connected with print and electronic media. With over 150 articles to choose from (and more on the way), we've worked to create a truly useful resource."

NASA. (1996). *Global Quest II: Teaching with the Internet.* [Video]. Washington, DC: Author.

This video, sponsored by NASA's IITA K–12 Internet Initiative, is an excellent introduction to the use of the Internet as an aid to doing PBL. (Available from NASA Ames Research Center, Moffett Field, CA 94035.)

National Foundation for the Improvement of Education. (1997). *Foundations for the road ahead: Project-based learning and information technologies.* Washington, DC: Author.

Most teachers give some open-ended assignments that provide students with a degree of choice and that extend over a considerable period of time. Such student activities are examples of PBL. IT increases the versatility and value of PBL as a curriculum tool. IT can help create a rich environment for individuals and teams to carry out in-depth projects that draw on multimedia and information resources from throughout the world. Research and evaluation for the Road Ahead Program were carried out by the International Society for Technology in Education in a project directed by David Moursund.

National Standards, Assessments, and Reports. [Online]. Accessed 5/28/02: **http://otec.uoregon.edu/national_standards.htm**

Quoting from the Web site: "National K–12 standards have been developed in many different curriculum areas. In many of the curriculum areas, the national standards include specific reference to IT. National assessment is an important but often controversial vehicle in educational policy and politics. From time to time, a national report is developed by some 'commission' or other high-level group, and such reports may have a significant impact on our educational system."

Norman, Donald. (1990). *The design of everyday things.* New York: Doubleday.

Donald Norman is a cognitive scientist and a prolific, witty author. He has a high level of expertise in the domain of human-machine interfaces and is interested in both noncomputer and computer-based human-machine interfaces. This book provides an excellent introduction to the design of such everyday tools as doors, drawers, and stoves. He gives many examples of poorly designed tools for humans.

Norman, Donald. (1993). *Things that make us smart: Defending human attributes in the age of machines.* Reading, MA: Addison-Wesley.

This publication provides a superb discussion of the roles of technology in enhancing our intellectual capabilities. Norman emphasizes that poorly designed machines can make us feel dumb and prevent us from using our intelligence effectively (see the previous entry).

Norman, Donald. *February 2001 interview of Donald Norman.* [Online]. Accessed 5/28/02: **www.elearningpost.com/elthemes/norman.asp**

Donald Norman has made significant contributions to the field of designing software and other products. He has written a number of quite readable and interesting books. This interview includes a focus on learner-centered instruction or user-centered design, and on problem-based learning. Quoting from the interview:

elearningpost: "In all your books, you have emphasized the need to put the user at the center of all design initiatives. User-centric design has been your mantra. Now, with e-learning, there is a similar need to put the learner at the center of all design initiatives. Going with your experience as the President of UNext Learning Systems, what are some of the issues one needs to consider in order to adopt a learner-centric approach?"

Donald Norman: "We have to start at several places. The traditional course is run by a professor, an instructor, who organizes the course material in some logical method and gives lecture materials and assigns readings. This is an approach that we can call either "teacher-centric," or maybe "content-centric." And it fails to take into account the way people learn. The first step in learner-centric is to understand how learning takes place. Much modern research in cognitive science shows that people learn by doing. So it is very important that people learn not by reading a book, and not by listening to a lecture, but by doing tasks that can engage the mind."

"The second point to understand is that when you read or listen to something, what do you learn from it? The answer: It depends on the goals that you have. In a traditional course, the students do not know why they are reading the material. They may be reading because the professor said 'read this material.' What we try to do in UNext is we give the students a problem to solve. Now when students read the material, they know the goal; they are trying to find the information that will solve their problem."

Oregon Technology in Education Council (OTEC). [Online]. Accessed 5/28/02: **http://otec.uoregon.edu**

OTEC is a nonprofit grassroots organization dedicated to improving Oregon's formal and informal education at all levels through the appropriate use of IT. OTEC includes a number of "Virtual Communities" of IT-using educators from all levels of education.

Papert, S. (1993). *The children's machine: Rethinking school in the age of the computer.* New York: Basic Books.

Papert is well known for his work as a computer scientist at the Massachusetts Institute of Technology. He is still better known for his work as a computer educator, particularly in the Logo field. His philosophy of education is built on and extends the work of Piaget. The focus is on hands-on, discovery-based learning by doing, and it takes advantage of Logo and similar powerful new learning environments. It can be described as an adaptation of the ideas of constructivism to a kids-oriented computer programming environment.

Pea, R.D. (1985). Beyond amplification: Using the computer to reorganize mental functioning. *Educational Psychologist, 20*(4), 167–182.

This article focuses on the difference between the rather mundane uses of computers to help solve problems and accomplish cognitive tasks and the more profound, deeper uses of computers. At the time the article was written, most cognitive uses of computers were rather superficial. For example, using a computer as a word processor or as a high-speed calculator is considered to be "amplification" of current cognitive processes. Pea speculates on possible types of cognitive uses of computers that move beyond amplification and lead to major changes in the way we think about, approach, and solve problems.

Penuel, W. R., & Means, B. (1999). *Observing classroom processes in project-based learning using multimedia: A tool for evaluators.* [Online]. Accessed 5/28/02: **www.ed.gov/Technology/TechConf/1999/whitepapers/paper3.html**

Quoting from the paper: "Abstract: This paper discusses methods for observing changes in classroom processes in project-based classrooms using multimedia technology. The tool was used as part of a five-year evaluation of a local Technology Innovation Challenge Grant program called Challenge 2000: Multimedia Project. In the paper, we discuss the design of the observation tool and present findings about the differences in classroom processes between Multimedia Project classrooms and comparison classrooms. Project classrooms, we found, are more likely to be learner-centered and engage students in long-term, complex assignments.:"

"There are seven components of the Project-Based Learning Using Multimedia model. Projects are expected to: (1) Be anchored in core curriculum; multidisciplinary; (2) Involve students in sustained effort over time; (3) Involve student decision-making; (4) Be collaborative; (5) Have a clear real-world connection; (6) Use systematic assessment: both along the way and end product; and (7) Take advantage of multimedia as a communication tool.

Performance Assessment (September 1993). [Online]. Accessed 5/28/02: **www.ed.gov/pubs/OR/ConsumerGuides/perfasse.html**

This U.S. Office of Education report provides a brief but excellent introduction to performance assessment.

Perkins, D. (1992). *Smart schools: Better thinking and learning for every child.* New York: Free Press.

David Perkins is codirector (along with Howard Gardner) of Project Zero, a major center for research on children's learning, at Harvard University. During the past few decades there has been an immense amount of research that provides evidence on how to improve education. Perkins' book summarizes and analyzes that research carefully and systematically.

Perkins, D. (1995). *Outsmarting IQ: The emerging science of learnable intelligence.* New York: Free Press.

This book provides a careful analysis of possible definitions of intelligence and how IQ is measured. Three different but closely related components of intelligence are explored: neural intelligence, experiential intelligence, and reflexive intelligence.

Arguments are presented to support the contention that all three components of IQ can change. In particular, appropriately designed education can increase experiential and reflexive IQ. This book also has a major focus on transfer of learning, with particular emphasis on the high-road/low-road theory of transfer developed by Perkins and Salomon in 1987.

PERT, CPM, and GANTT. [Online]. Accessed 5/28/02:
http://studentweb.tulane.edu/~mtruill/dev-pert.html

This Web site provides a nice overview of three project-planning methodologies. It is taken from Martin E. Modell's A Professional's Guide to Systems Analysis, (2nd. ed.), McGraw Hill, 1996.

Polya, George. (1957). *How to solve it: A new aspect of mathematical method* (2nd ed.). Princeton, NJ: Princeton University Press.

This book is considered a classic in the field of learning and teaching about problem solving. The emphasis is on strategies and meta-strategies applicable over a wide range of math problems. A number of the strategies discussed are applicable in areas outside of mathematics and thus contribute to transfer of learning to other fields. Examples include breaking a problem into subproblems and relating a problem to other problems encountered in the past.

President's Committee of Advisors on Science and Technology (PCAST). Panel on Educational Technology. (1997, March). *Report to the President on the use of technology to strengthen K–12 education in the United States.* [Online]. Accessed 5/28/02:
www.ostp.gov/PCAST/pcast.html

This report, prepared by a blue-ribbon committee, contains a careful analysis of research literature on instructional uses of IT. There is a substantial emphasis on constructivism as one of the important underlying theories. The report contains recommendations to policy makers (including the President of the United States) on needed research and implementation efforts.

Program Evaluation and Review Technique (PERT). [Online]. Accessed 5/28/02:
www.uwf.edu/coehelp/studentaccounts/rnew/perthome.html?ti2Xdw=www.uwf.edu/~coehelp/studentaccounts/rnew/perthome.html

Quoting from the Web site: "PERT, developed by the United States Department of Defense as a management tool for complex military projects, is an acronym for Program Evaluation and Review Technique...."

"PERT charts can become very complex if detailed networks exist, but they force the manager to contemplate personnel assignments for the project in detail. To demonstrate best- and worst-case project scenarios, most PERT charts identify three time estimates: most optimistic, most pessimistic, and most realistic. PERT charts are very useful in large, complex studies where overlooking details may create unresolvable problems. PERT charts are frequently used within an organization for detailed evaluation planning. The critical path of a PERT chart highlights important interim deadlines that must be met if the overall evaluation study is to be completed on time.

Problem-Based Learning Clearinghouse. [Online]. Accessed 5/28/02:
www.mis4.udel.edu/Pbl/#

Quoting from the Web site: "Welcome to the PBL Clearinghouse, a collection of problems and articles to assist educators in using problem-based learning. The problems and articles are peer reviewed by PBL experts in the disciplinary content areas. Teaching notes and supplemental materials accompany each problem, providing insights and strategies that are innovative and classroom-tested. Access to the clearinghouse collection is limited to educators who register via an online application, but is free and carries no obligation."

Project-Based Instruction in Mathematics for the Liberal Arts. [Online]. Accessed 5/28/02: **www.uscs.edu/~mulmer/PBI_Index.shtml**

Quoting from the Web site: The purpose of this Web site is to provide projects and resources for instructors and students who wish to teach and learn college mathematics or postalgebra high school mathematics via project-based instruction. This site is evolving, so check it often for improvements. Project-Based Instruction in Mathematics for the Liberal Arts (PBI-MLA) is a relatively new program at the University of South Carolina, Spartanburg. In its fifth year, it enjoys a 30 percent higher success rate than do traditional textbook-driven sections of college mathematics.

Project-Based Learning with Multimedia :Multimedia Project Scoring Rubric: Scoring Guidelines. [Online]. Accessed 5/28/02: **http://pblmm.k12.ca.us/PBLGuide/MMrubric.htm**

This provides a one-page table using a 5-point rubric for each of the three components: multimedia, collaboration, and content of a project. This is based on the idea that one might want to assess a project on these three criteria.

Project-Based Science. [Online]. Accessed 5/28/02 **www.umich.edu/~pbsgroup/**

Quoting from the Web site: "Project-Based Science (PBS) is an effort that began in 1991 at the University of Michigan School of Education. It was originally funded by the National Science Foundation, and currently involves hundreds of K–12 science teachers in Michigan. The goal of the PBS group is to improve the way science classes are taught by involving students in finding solutions to authentic questions through extended inquiry, collaboration, and use of technology...."

"Project-Based Science organizes science class around a driving question. Everything the class does is focused on answering that question: investigations, computer work, library research, class discussions, and student-designed experiments."

"Investigations: Students pursue solutions to authentic problems by asking and refining questions, debating ideas, making predictions, designing plans and/or experiments, gathering information, collecting and analyzing data, drawing conclusions, and communicating their ideas and findings to others."

"Artifacts: These are the products of the student, which represent their knowledge and understanding of the driving question."

"Collaboration: In a Project-Based Science classroom, students discuss and try out their ideas and challenge the ideas of others. Telecommunications allow students to interact with a wider community of other students, and outside science experts to share information, data, resources, and ideas.

"Technology: Using technology in Project-Based Science makes the environment more authentic to students because the computer provides access to data and information, expands interaction and collaboration with others via networks, promotes laboratory investigation, and emulates tools experts use to produce artifacts."

Projects for Public Spaces. [Online]. Accessed 5/28/02: **www.pps.org/tcb/about.htm**

> Quoting from the Web site: "At Project for Public Spaces, we believe it's important to highlight accomplishments of young people. In our work around the U.S., we witness all too often how young people are shunned and treated almost like undesirables by the owners and managers of public spaces. On top of that, there seems to be continuous press coverage of negative activities undertaken by teens. This makes it even more important to tell stories of youth who are doing positive things to improve their communities. In addition, these examples of teens' success can provide inspiration to other youth who are struggling to make a difference, and trying to create public places that are comfortable for them and their peers—places where they have a sense of ownership and involvement."

> "We are a nonprofit organization dedicated to helping people of all ages create the kinds of places that build communities. We achieve this through technical assistance, training, research, and education—as well as programs in parks, plazas and central squares; transportation; public buildings; and architecture and public markets. Since our founding in 1975, we have worked in over 1,000 communities, within the U.S. and abroad, helping people to grow their public spaces into vital community places."

Rogers, E. M. (1995). *Diffusion of innovations.* New York: The Free Press.

> This is the definitive book summarizing and analyzing the adoption of innovations. Why are some innovations widely adopted and others rejected? Rogers draws on the research (consisting of nearly 4,000 published papers) as he explores successes and failures.

Rothman, R. (1995). *Measuring up: Standards, assessment, and school reform.* San Francisco, CA: Jossey-Bass.

> Written for the educated layperson, this book provides good coverage of the advantages, disadvantages, and issues underlying alternative assessment. It provides a number of examples of schools and school districts that have implemented alternative forms of assessment.

Rubrics and Self-Assessment Project from Project Zero. [Online]. Accessed 5/28/02: **http://pzweb.harvard.edu/Research/StuSA.htm**

> Quoting from the Web site: "Scoring rubrics are among the most popular innovations in education (Goodrich, 1997a; Jensen, 1995; Ketter, 1997; Luft, 1997; Popham, 1997). However, little research on their design and their effectiveness has been undertaken. Moreover, few of the existing research and development efforts have focused on the ways in which rubrics can serve the purposes of learning and cognitive development as well as the demands of evaluation and accountability. The two studies that made up the Project Zero's research focused on the effect of instructional rubrics and rubric-referenced self-assessment on the development of seventh- and eighth-grade students' writing skills and their understandings of the qualities of good writing."

Salomon, G., & Perkins, D. (1988, September). Teaching for transfer. *Educational Leadership,* pp. 22–32.

> Salomon and Perkins developed the high-road/low-road theory of transfer of learning. This article provides a good overview of the domain of transfer of learning and how to teach transfer. It also contains an extensive bibliography, so it is a good starting point if you want to study the research on this topic.

Sandholtz, J. H., Ringstaff, C., & Dwyer, D. C. (1997). *Teaching with technology: Creating student-centered classrooms.* New York: Teachers College Press.

> This reports on a 10-year research study of the Apple Classroom of Tomorrow (ACOT) school sites. Both the students and teachers participating in these studies were provided with a microcomputer to use at home and a microcomputer to use at school. A variety of schools participated. The book provides an excellent analysis of positive and negative effects at these high-density computer sites from approximately 1985 to 1995. It contains a foreword by Larry Cuban, who observes that "few books can engage both doubters and true believers simultaneously. This is one of the few that will."

Stamford Problem-Based Learning Initiative. [Online]. Accessed 5/28/02: **www.samford.edu/pbl/pbl_main.html**

> Quoting from the Web site: "The Center [for Problem-Based Learning] is an arm of The Samford PBL Initiative, a project supported by The Pew Charitable Trusts and was designed to answer the following questions: (1) Does PBL improve student learning and skill development?; (2) Can PBL be successful in conventionally funded higher education?; (3) How can colleges and universities most effectively integrate PBL? This Web site serves as a clearinghouse of information about PBL in undergraduate and professional education."

Sternberg, R. (1988). *The triarchic mind: A new theory of human intelligence.* New York: Penguin Books.

> This book provides an excellent overview of the history of and work on the attempts to define and test intelligence. Sternberg argues that previous theories are inadequate, and he presents a three-part definition of intelligence. He is a strong supporter of the idea that intelligence can be improved.

Sternberg, R. (1997). *Successful intelligence: How practical and creative intelligence determine success in life.* New York: Penguin Putnam.

> This book, written for beginners, updates the ideas in Sternberg's The Triarchic Mind (see the previous entry). It presents a detailed overview of the flaws in the current definitions and measurements of intelligence. The focus is on providing a practical, useful definition and set of measurements. This book provides an excellent starting point for readers who want to explore this field.

Stites, Regie. (1998, January). *Evaluation of project-based learning.* [Online]. Accessed 5/28/02: **http://pblmm.k12.ca.us/PBLGuide/pblresch.htm**

> Quoting the first two paragraphs of this brief report from SRI, International: "Researchers have investigated the impact of project-based learning (PBL) in a wide variety of educational contexts ranging from early childhood education to medical and legal education. PBL (and related instructional approaches) has generally been shown to be effective in increasing student motivation and in improving student problem-solving and higher order thinking skills."

> "Problem-based learning practices (that share most of the features of PBL in K–12 settings) have been used for many years in higher education (Barrows, 1996; Schmidt, 1994; Williams, 1992). Recently, two reviews have summarized more than 20 years of evaluations of PBL in medical education (Albanese & Mitchell, 1993; Vernon & Blake, 1993). These studies show that medical students in PBL programs perform as well as students in traditional programs on conventional tests of knowledge. In addition, PBL medical students do better on tests of clinical problem-solving skills."

TERC. [Online]. Accessed 5/28/02: **www.terc.edu**

Quoting from the Web site: "Founded in 1965, TERC is a not-for-profit education research and development organization in Cambridge, Massachusetts. TERC's mission is to improve mathematics, science, and technology teaching and learning. TERC works at the edges of current theory and practice to: (1) contribute to understanding of learning and teaching; (2) foster professional development; (3) develop applications of new technologies; (4) create curricula and other products; and (5) support school reform."

Using Hypermedia to Facilitate Problem-Based Learning. [Online]. Accessed 5/28/02: **www.edb.utexas.edu/mmresearch/Students97/Hemstreet/**

This 1997 Web site provides a good introduction to the theory and practice of problem-based learning.

Wiburg, K., & Carter, B. (1994). Thinking with computers. *The Computing Teacher, 22*(1), 7–10.

This is the first of a two-part column entitled "Research Windows." It discusses recent research on the effects of educational technology on improving problem solving.

Wiggins, Grant. (1990). The case for authentic assessment. *ERIC Digest.* [Online]. Accessed 5/28/02: **http://ericae.net/db/edo/ED328611.htm**

Quoting from the Web site: "Assessment is authentic when we directly examine student performance on worthy intellectual tasks. Traditional assessment, by contract, relies on indirect or proxy 'items'—efficient, simplistic substitutes from which we think valid inferences can be made about the student's performance at those valued challenges. Do we want to evaluate student problem-posing and problem-solving in mathematics? experimental research in science? speaking, listening, and facilitating a discussion? doing document-based historical inquiry? thoroughly revising a piece of imaginative writing until it 'works' for the reader? Then let our assessment be built out of such exemplary intellectual challenges...."

"Authentic assessments attend to whether the student can craft polished, thorough, and justifiable answers, performances, or products. Conventional tests typically only ask the student to select or write correct responses—irrespective of reasons. (There is rarely an adequate opportunity to plan, revise, and substantiate responses on typical tests, even when there are open-ended questions). As a result,

"Authentic assessment achieves validity and reliability by emphasizing and standardizing the appropriate criteria for scoring such (varied) products; traditional testing standardizes objective 'items' and, hence, the (one) right answer for each."

Wiggins, Grant. (1993a). *Assessing student performance.* San Francisco, CA: Jossey-Bass.

Wiggins is a leading researcher and author on authentic assessment. This comprehensive book provides the solid background needed by anyone seriously exploring authentic assessment.

Wiggins, Grant. (1993b, November). Assessment: Authenticity, context, and validity. *Phi Delta Kappan,* pp. 200–214.

This article consists of materials abstracted from Wiggins' book *Assessing Student Performance* (see previous entry).

Wiggins, Grant. (1996–1997, December-January). Practicing what we preach in designing authentic assessments. *Educational Leadership,* pp. 18–25.

This article provides an analysis of effective practices in developing authentic assessment materials. The emphasis is on using authentic assessment techniques in the process of developing assessments.

Willis, J. W., & Mehlinger, H. D. (1996). Information technology and teacher education. In Sikula, J., Buttery, T. J., & Guyton, E. (Eds.), *Handbook of research on teacher education* (2nd ed.) (pp. 978–1029). New York: Simon & Schuster Macmillan.

This material provides a comprehensive survey of IT in teacher education. The bibliography contains approximately 300 items. While the material is based mainly on the research literature from 1987 to 1994, it also contains a historical perspective and a careful analysis of constructivism in teaching, which is contrasted with behaviorism and didactic methods of instruction.

Yoder, S., & Smith, I. (1995). *Lookin' good! The elements of document design for beginners.* Eugene, OR: International Society for Technology in Education.

Designed for beginners and casual computer users from age 14 to adult, this book will help the user realize the power of the computer as a production studio for print documents of professional quality. It is a good resource for those who want to learn how to take advantage of the powerful desktop-publication features of a modern computer.

index

A

action research 16

amplification 18, 95-96

anchored instruction 36

artificial intelligence 88, 90, 111

AskERIC 108

assessment xi, 7-9, 12, 14, 15, 17, 19, 30, 40, 48, 57, 58, 60, 62, 65-78, 80, 82-84, 95-98
  authentic xii, 7, 14, 65-67, 70, 73, 74, 78, 83, 85
  authentic content xii, 14, 65
  environmental 13
  goals 66
  high stakes 66, 67
  needs 47
  peer 6, 15, 61, 73, 85
  performance-based 65, 66, 78
  portfolio 66
  self xii, 6, 12, 13, 15, 19, 61, 72, 73, 78, 85
  valid, reliable, fair 9, 26, 65

authentic educational goal 58

B

back-to-basics movement 39-40

BASIC 79

Bereiter, Carl 110

big ideas 7, 27-29

Blumenfeld, Phyllis C. 36

brain theory 16, 88

C

calculator 17, 19, 28, 90, 94, 96, 97, 101, 105, 111
  graphing 32-33, 94, 96
  handheld 28, 90, 111

Civil War 69-70

classroom management 13

collaboration 12, 18

collaborative learning 61

collaborative problem solving 37

community of scholars 7, 67

computer model 96, 106

computer science 90

computer-assisted design 90

computer-assisted learning 18, 68

computer-assisted learning (CAL) 91, 97

computer-assisted research 91

constructivism xi, xii, 12, 14, 15, 16, 35, 36, 88

cooperative learning 12, 37

curriculum design 27

D

Dewey, John 16

discovery-based learning xii